KUDOS
for the Documentary
"The Conservation Game"

"'The Conservation Game' won the Social Justice Award for Documentary Film at this year's Santa Barbara International Film Festival. What is so beautiful about the award is that it reflects the growing awareness and recognition in our society that the treatment of animals is a social justice issue that intersects with just about everything!"

"If Tiger King is the tabloid take on the big cat story, 'The Conservation Game' is the Pro Publica version. Will potentially change the animal entertainment industry forever."

"In this case, Tiger King is Rosencrantz and Guildenstern Are Dead, and 'The Conservation Game' is Hamlet. The farce is good for a few laughs, but the tragedy has more staying power."

– Film Threat

PRAISE
For *White Magic*

"Tim Harrison's life work has been education, compassion, empathy, understanding and safety. There is no one more willing to step up to make a difference for animals despite the cost or risk. He's someone you always want in your corner fighting the good fight."
—Cheryl Tuller, Executive Director, WildCat Ridge Sanctuary

"*White Magic* will ensure that the most exploited tigers in America finally have their overdue 'Blackfish' moment they need and deserve. Harrison pierces the fiction that exploiters have been relying on for decades to profit off public misconception that there's conservation value in white tiger photo ops or breeding programs."
—Carney Anne Nasser, Esq., Director, Animal Welfare Clinic, Michigan State University College of Law

"*White Magic* reveals the 'Con' in 'Conservation'—when the only thing these zoos and roadside attractions are rehabilitating are their own bank accounts. Read this book to learn, act, and save the tiger."
—Steve Winter, award-winning *BBC Wildlife* photographer, National Geographic photographer

"Harrison has pulled back the curtain on the horror behind the U.S. industry in 'snow tigers.' He dispels the myth that this is conservation of a species, revealing through deep research and eloquent writing that 'tiger mills' bang out these heavily inbred cats strictly for entertainment, for tourist photo-ops and for backyard pets. He details the history of their popularity, sale, the suffering these animals endure, the public safety issues—and offers solutions to end this cruel industry."

—Sharon Guynup, National Geographic Explorer, Global Fellow, Woodrow Wilson International Center for Scholars

WHITE MAGIC

Tim Harrison

Orange frazer Press
Wilmington, Ohio

ISBN 978-1949248-029
Copyright©2021 Tim Harrison
All Rights Reserved

No part of this publication may be reproduced in any material form (including photocopying or storing in any medium by electronic means and whether or not transiently or incidentally to some other use of this publication) without the written permission of the copyright holder except in accordance with the provisions of Title 17 of the United States Code.

Published by:
Orange Frazer Press
Box 214
37½ West Main Street
Wilmington, Ohio 45177

For price and shipping information, call: 937.382.3196
Or visit: www.orangefrazer.com

Cover photo by: WildCat Ridge Sanctuary copyright 2013
Photographer: Karine Aigner (www.karineaigner.com)
Book and Cover design by: Kelly Schutte and
Orange Frazer Press

Library of Congress Control Number: 2021938099

This publication is meant as a source of valuable information for the reader, and the publisher and the author have made every effort to ensure that the information in this book was correct at press time. While this publication is designed to provide accurate information in regard to the subject matter covered, the publisher and the author assume no responsibility for errors, inaccuracies, omissions, or any other inconsistencies herein and hereby disclaim any liability to any party for any loss, damage, or disruption caused by errors or omissions, whether such errors or omissions result from negligence, accident, or any other cause.

Opinions expressed in this publication are the sole responsibility of the author and Outreach for Animals.

First Printing

DEDICATION

To Bill Randolph, my long-time friend, currently serving as proofreader, sounding board, confidant, and unofficial quasi-editor throughout the compilation of this book.

To Russ Clear, my friend, partner, and fellow wildlife warrior, who has helped me as much as he has the big cats we have rescued.

To Renee Radziwon-Chapman, who gave her life selflessly protecting and caring for big cats.

In memory of Matt Hieb, a good friend and supporter of our mission. If it wasn't for Matt, there would be no books, there would be no documentaries. He will not only be remembered, he will be missed.

And to all those big cats and other exotic animals who gave their lives in man's pursuit of his own selfish pleasures.

ACKNOWLEDGMENTS

During my years working with big cats, I have had the pleasure to work with some amazing organizations: Lions, Tigers and Bears-Alpine, California (Bobby Brink); Black Pine Animal Sanctuary-Albion, Indiana (Lori Gagen); Wild Cat Ridge Sanctuary-Scotts Mills, Oregon (Cheryl and Mike Tuller); The Wildcat Sanctuary-Sandstone, Minnesota (Tammy Thies); Turpentine Creek Wildlife Refuge-Eureka Springs, Arkansas (Tanya and Scott Smith); The Wild Animal Sanctuary-Keenesburg, Colorado (Pat Craig); Big Cat Rescue-Tampa, Florida (Carole and Howard Baskin); Tiger Haven-Kingston, Tennessee (Mary Haven); and all the members of the Big Cat Sanctuary Alliance.

A special thanks to Rus Muntz, Keith Gad, Mike Webber, and Bill Cacciolfi for all their hard work and support of Outreach for Animals.

To my wife, Patricia, thank you for helping me pursue the impossible and loving me all the way.

CONTENTS

	INTRODUCTION	*xv*
1	White Tigers, White Lies	3
2	What is a White Tiger?	8
3	Mutants	14
4	Myths, Facts, and Confusion	18
5	Nikki	24
6	CONservation	30
7	Cats, Celebrities, and Cops	37
8	Yuki	49
9	Nikita and Nora	59
10	Tiger in a Box	66
11	How Much is that Tiger in the Window?	70
12	Cash for Cats	74
13	Canned Cats	79
14	The Good, the Bad, and the Ugly	84
15	Character Assassination	89
16	Where are the Laws?	98
	EPILOGUE	*105*
	APPENDIX	*111*
	LEGISLATION	*119*
	INFORMED SOURCES, ORGANIZATIONS, AND SANCTUARIES	*127*
	ABOUT THE AUTHORS	*133*

INTRODUCTION
The Curse of the White Tiger

Images of the most misunderstood and abused animals on the planet are everywhere—on puzzles, calendars, posters, books, magazines, t-shirts, and television. Ask the average person what his or her favorite "wild" animal is, and many will say, the white tiger, the tiger used by magicians and popular TV animal educators "to educate" the public about "the plight of the tigers in Asia."

The Association of Zoos & Aquariums refers to them as "ambassador animals." And for all practical purposes, this means they are bred to be used as TV props to help alleged 'conservation' organizations get millions of dollars in donations. But what does the white tiger cub get out of this arrangement?

The cub gets shuffled around to different national TV shows and VIP photo parties, thrust into the glaring spotlights, all to the applause of excited spectators. Education? The sad reality is that it is all just entertainment.

In this book, the reader will be introduced to four white tigers that I have worked with, while meeting other big cats along the way: Nora, the sweetest big cat I have ever met; Nikita, the most vicious one; Como, who had the most horrific story; and Yuki—the most mysterious story of all.

They help explain the plight of the white tiger in the U.S. Their tales may make you angry, laugh, or cry. My experiences with them has turned my life around in ways I could never have imagined. In some cases, it has been a dream; in others, a nightmare.

My goal, when all the layers are peeled back, remains to—hopefully—end the myths that have grown up around these tragic creatures and to showcase the truth behind the camera lights. Inside, you will be introduced to the true white tiger, and you will probably never again look at white tigers in the same way.

What is a white tiger? Why they are white? Are they really a rare breed? Why are they called "Royal White tigers?" Why do the Association of Zoos and Aquariums no longer support the breeding of white tigers? What does it mean when someone says "White Magic?" Does the uncontrolled breeding of white tigers really help the Bengal tigers in the wild?

These questions will be answered, and there will also be answers to other questions you may never have thought to ask before. In the end you'll wonder, perhaps, why you hadn't.

WHITE MAGIC

1
White Tigers, White Lies

In my formative years my parents always told me that the fireworks show and local parade was for my birthday. When I started first grade, I figured out that the festivities were not for me alone. And just as I was slow to learn the truth behind the Fourth of July, so was it that over time I would come to realize the much less romantic truth behind white tigers.

On October 30, 1958, a litter of four white cubs was born to Mohan and Radha, at the Maharaja of Rewa's Palace of Govindgarh. Mohan was the first white tiger to sire cubs in captivity, and Radha's litter was made up of three females, Rani, Mohini, Sukeshi, and a male named Raja. Mohini—whose name meant "Enchantress"—was bought by John W. Klugh, an American billionaire who paid the Maharaja of Rewa $10,000 and gifted Mohini to the National Zoo in Washington, DC. She came to America in December of 1960, overnighting at the Bronx and Philadelphia zoos before taking up residence at her new home in Washington. She was believed to be one of only seven white tigers in the world and, said the *Washington Post*, the only one outside of India.

Mohini, who'd been purchased by Klugh as a gift to the children of America, almost didn't make the trip because India had banned the exportation of white tigers. (It wished to monopolize its proprietorship for the tourist industry.) Mohini was permitted to leave only because President Eisenhower personally intervened with Prime Minister Nehru.

A tiger named Sampson was acquired to be Mohini's mate, and the pair had litters in 1964 and 1966, but not without a little domestic violence. Sampson bit off part of Mohini's ear on their first introduction, the implication being that the course of true love is seldom tranquil. Mohini's daughter, Kesari, was the most important cub out of the litters. Kesari was orange but carried the white gene, and this made her responsible for carrying on the white tiger line.

Mohini's arrival in America began the breeding of the most popular exotic wild animal in history. She appeared in newsreels and specials, toured the country, visited with the president, and became the most popular animal in the U.S. The zoo finally built her a large natural habitat, but when she was released into it she chose a small perimeter area of about twelve-by-twelve-feet, the size of her old cage. She never left these imaginary confines and after her death, she became a much-cited lesson about the perils of conditioning.

She died on April 2, 1979, at the age of 20, which according to researcher Mary Ann Howell is the human equivalent of a hundred years. The *Washington Post* in its obituary relived her arrival in America: "Think how she felt, the harem beauty transported against her will from a fairy-tale existence in the Mahajarah's harem courtyard to a barbarous country far away. No wonder she was in a foul mood; all those cameras flashing, all that noise. President or no president, White House or no White House. She growled. 'Look,' President Dwight D. Eisenhower (according to press accounts) replied, 'I'm not going to get in that cage.'"

The late Ted Reed, director of the National Zoo during Mohini's time there put her death in perspective when he said, "It's difficult to say how much the zoo owes that cat and her cubs. They drew attention to the facility and made all our recent improvements so much easier."

Mohini's skull, skin, and skeleton were preserved at the Smithsonian's National Museum of Natural History where they remain to this day, although they are not displayed. They are actually in storage in a warehouse in Maryland, and the remains of the most famous tiger of all time are hidden away, not in the forest of India but in containers in Maryland. In her lifetime, Mohini brought money and fame to the National Zoo, yet her legacy is a box hidden away in a warehouse.

Would Mohini have given up all that fame just to run free in the wild? Movie stars have a choice of being in the public eye. Mohini the Enchantress did not.

From my budding awareness of white tigers at the age of five to the media exploitation of white tigers during my lifetime—and the recent awakening by the Association of Zoos and Aquariums that white tigers will no longer be bred—my thinking about these beautiful mutant Bengal tigers has dramatically changed. My discovery of the exploitation of the tigers has had a profound and long-lasting effect on me.

From an early age, I knew white tigers were not being bred for the survival of the Bengal tiger species in the wild. I had a teacher in my elementary school who explained that animals bred and raised in captivity rarely, if ever, were reintroduced into the wild. As an example, she used raccoons, a common wild animal raised by people in our area of the country. She explained that once a wild raccoon kit was captured and raised in a human environment, it could never return safely to the wild.

What she taught us was that once the kit matures and imprints with its human parents, it will not fear humans. The raccoon would then approach all humans and expect food or physical contact. But most prudent people walking through the woods would be frightened if a raccoon approached them, and so in this fashion a human-imprinted wild animal would endanger itself.

It is also extremely rare that a person keeps a raccoon as a pet through maturity. For when a raccoon becomes sexually mature, its natural instincts take over and its tendency is to turn on its owners. The raccoon does not need the human anymore. So the raccoon is released back into the wild, which is a death sentence for a once-beloved pet.

It didn't take long for me to take the lessons I learned from my fourth-grade teacher about raccoons and apply them to tigers. As I grew up and traveled the world, I learned the countries that tigers come from would never allow a hand-raised tiger imprinted with humans to be released into their wild areas. Imagine a four-hundred-pound Bengal tiger, imprinted with people, loose in India. The tiger would walk up to humans without fear. Whatever might happen next would probably be good for neither human nor tiger.

The tiger, like the raccoon, becomes sexually mature and no longer needs the human. Almost overnight, the tiger becomes a stranger in its own land, whether it's in an accredited zoo or someone's backyard. The tiger goes from being handled for photo opportunities and sleeping in its human's bed to becoming too large and scaring the human caretakers. Such animals are placed permanently in cages or backyard corn cribs to live out their lives. One day, the tiger is sleeping and playing together with his adopted family, and the next day he is placed in a cage to walk in a constant circle, showing signs of extreme stress. I call these tigers "broken animals." To do this to a dog or housecat is considered animal cruelty.

Human imprinting on these tigers condemns them to a life in captivity, because predatory wild animals raised by humans do not survive successfully in the wild. No tiger or big cat born and raised in captivity has been successfully released in the wild, much to the chagrin of those who are told tigers raised in captivity are raised to stop the decimation of wild tigers.

They do not know what happens to these animals once the media push is done and the cameras are off.

Stay tuned for the real story.

2

What is a White Tiger?

"White tigers are the result of a genetic anomaly that occurs so rarely that only twelve have been confirmed in the wild in over one hundred years."
—Professor Carney Anne Nasser

The modern day white tiger was born into slavery and died in captivity, all from being loved too much. These tigers are being loved to death, all under the guise of a romantic-sounding name whispered with equal measures of reverence, sarcasm, and even disdain—*White Magic*.

White Magic is industry shorthand for the effect white tigers have on the public—and the mystique they embody. White Magic is both born from, and perpetuates, the mythos of the white tigers. And it is White Magic that ultimately leads to their abuse and death.

When I first heard the words "White Magic," I had to investigate its origins. I had met a group of circus entertainers using a white tiger cub for "photo opportunities" at a local circus, and I walked up and asked them if they ever heard the term "White Magic." The older circus performer laughed and said, "Yes." He said "White Magic" was a kind of slang created by insiders who sold, exploited, and made money off white tigers. "Watch the faces of the people in line, waiting for their opportunity to hold, and get a photo with a white tiger cub," he said. "That's White Magic."

So before we delve further into the world of white tigers—and "White Magic"—let's dispel some of the myths. First of all, these beautiful creatures aren't a separate species, or even a subspecies. They are simply the result of, as *Scientific American* explained, "a rare but naturally occurring genetic variant within the wild Bengal population." That is, white tigers are Bengal tigers, differing from their orange-and-striped family members only because of their odd genetic imprint. They are not albino. Neither are they some Siberian species that evolved to live in the snow.

Explains *Scientific American*, "The white tiger's distinguishing characteristic arises from a single mutation, the substitution of one amino acid for another—valine for alanine—in the 'solute carrier' protein geneticists call SLC45A2. Its job is basically to transfer specific molecules across cellular barriers."

The anomaly of these tigers, where the orange coat becomes white, happens only when a tiger inherits two copies of what is called "the recessive variant." *Both* parents must carry this gene for the white color, and its occurrence has been estimated at no more than one in ten thousand births. Hence the rarity of the white tiger in nature.

When scientists from Peking University compared the DNA of several white tigers and orange ones, all related, they eventually focused on seven genes that always differed between the two. And finally they arrived at the gene known by its number—SLC45A2—which is involved in the production of melanin (even if no one knows exactly how). But it *is* known that it, and its variations, appear to be linked to everything from the pale skin of modern Europeans to light skin and hair in mice, chickens, horses, and even humans.

I once saw two white tigers from the same litter, with matching coloration, sent to two different facilities. After a year, I visited them. One white tiger seemed duller in color, not as radiant as her brother who was a brilliant white. I found out from a researcher that this is caused by enzymes that react to temperature differences.

This temperature difference causes the darkening of particular points on the fur when it gets cold. It might have been caused by the fact that the female white tiger spent less time outside in the winter. White tigers produce a mutated form of tyrosinase, which is a substance involved in the process of melanin production. This group of pigments is responsible for skin pigmentation. Tyrosinase produced in white tigers is a mutated form that functions only at temperatures below 37 degrees Celsius (98.6 Fahrenheit). Siamese cats and California White rabbits demonstrate this fact. When temperatures get cold, their ears, face, limbs and tails darken. This natural phenomenon is called acromelanism.

The stunningly beautiful snow white tigers came about as a result of multiple breedings between brother and sister, Bhim and Sumita. This inbreeding took place at the Cincinnati Zoo. The snow white tiger coloration may have been caused by the gene coming from the tiger's ancestor, a half Siberian tiger named Tony. About a quarter of Bhim and Sumita's offspring had no stripes—only pure white fur.

The white tiger we know from zoos, circuses, magic acts, and photo opportunities all came from one male tiger—the Maharaja's captive white tiger, Mohan. It was his famous daughter, Mohini, who brought the line to America. And her daughter Kesari, was loaned to the Cincinnati Zoo where she became what was called "the founding matriarch of the white tiger collection there."

Even at that time, the price of a white tiger was said to be $60,000. Author David Quammen interviewed one of the Cincinnati Zoo's tiger curators and asked him the purpose of interbreeding a family line to produce so many white cubs. "It's marketing," the curator said. "It's popularity. It's a major source of income for continuing other programs here at the zoo."

The Cincinnati Zoo started its own white tiger breeding program, and its successful program of inbreeding produced a market for the cubs, which were then sold in zoos from Canada to Japan. By the 1980s, the Cincinnati Zoo was called "the world's leading purveyor of white tigers."

In 1983, the Cincinnati Zoo sold three white tigers—including the first pure white tiger cub (no stripes)—to Las Vegas magicians Siegfried and Roy. Their Las Vegas show made the white tigers (and cubs) its signature animal. This phenomenon established the market value for the white tiger cub. White tiger cubs with black stripes went for $30,000, the pure white cubs (no stripes) for $100,000. Siegfried and Roy's magic show became the fifth greatest headliner in the history of Las Vegas, edged out only by the likes of Liberace, The Rat Pack, Elvis, and Celine Dion. And their success was directly related to the white tigers.

Siegfried and Roy's act sold out for over twenty-five years, and led generations of Americans to fall in love with the white tiger. The public opinion of the white tiger as a pet or an endangered animal that they perpetuated caused a breeding binge that emerged from the zoo system and into the backyards of animal breeders, which became a lucrative business.

But in captivity, says Carole Baskin, CEO of Big Cat Rescue, inbred tiger parents produce only one white cub out of every four born—and eighty percent of the white cubs die from birth defects. Many tiger 'conservationists' think to get the one perfect white tiger cub, twenty-nine others are rejected as "not suitable for display." This over-breeding causes a disposable orange tiger population of hundreds, possibly thousands, just to produce the one desirable white tiger. And in the unsentimental world of tiger exploitation, "rejected" can mean anything from being killed to ending up in a roadside zoo. In truth, no one knows where they go. And they are not on the minds of the thousands of Siegfried and Roy fans.

The white tiger cubs tend to suffer from some level of birth defects: crossed eyes, cleft palates, spinal deformities, and club feet are sadly common from inbred white tiger cubs. Professor Carney Anne Nasser, currently director of the Animal Welfare Clinic at the Michigan College of Law, lists them as including the following: "crossed eyes, cleft palate, clubbed feet, kidney abnormalities, scoliosis, strabismus, blindness, vascular anomalies that inhibit the ability to feed and swallow, congenital defects in cranial and skull development, and diminished life expectancy." It is believed their brains do not always process images well, which means they bump into things before they learn to compensate, and they are sensitive to light.

The crossed eyes are caused by a gene responsible for the white coloration of the coat, and it also causes the optic nerve to be connected to the wrong side of the brain, which results in all white tigers being cross-eyed. This is a main reason why white tigers are favored over orange tigers in magic and circus acts: the white tigers with their diminished eyesight are more dependent on their trainers. Conversely, the genetic impairments make them unpredictable and potentially more dangerous. They react differently to stimulation and sometimes don't show the warning signs the orange tigers do.

Roy, of the Siegfried and Roy magic act, said after being attacked on stage by his white tiger, Montecore, that Montecore had never shown signs of aggression toward him before. His explanation was that Montecore sensed that he, Roy, was having a ministroke and was pulling him to safety. But male tigers have no paternal instincts, and they do not carry their young in their mouths. In fact, they sometimes kill them. Montecore would never have tried to carry Roy away in a protective manner. Montecore tried to kill him. It was only Montecore's lack of experience at killing that saved Roy's life.

Every time I see a performance or photo opportunity with a white tiger, I remember there were twenty-nine others that did not pass the audition. These tigers go back into the notorious breeding system, and if unable to breed, they will be sold in auction or dumped at some roadside zoo. Some may be rescued by an accredited sanctuary, but there are more white tiger rejects than sanctuaries to take them.

3

Mutants

"All white tigers in this country are generic and lack conservation value." —Doctors Ronald Tilson and Philip Nyhus

One of the country's foremost tiger experts is a woman named Carney Anne Nasser, director of Michigan State's Animal Welfare Clinic where she develops strategies for the legal interests and welfare of animals. If tigers had speed dial, Carney Anne Nasser would be at the top of the list.

Her peer-reviewed law journal article, "Welcome to the Jungle: How Loopholes in the Federal Endangered Species Act and Animal Welfare Act are Feeding a Tiger Crisis in America," published in 2016, draws from a wealth of study at the hands of the most notable scientists, researchers, breeders, and biologists in the field. In her succinct, clear-minded prose (something not always found in academic papers), she presents a powerful overview of the tiger in America, as well as poignantly spelling out the plight of white tigers.

Her essay—used as a template for exotic animal advocates nationwide—tells us of the astounding popularity of tigers (they're mascots for more than 1,400 sports teams in America, for instance), but it also informs us that the tiger's natural population in the last hundred years has declined by ninety-seven percent. Three of the nine tiger subspecies have completely vanished, and another exists only in captivity. According to tiger conservationists, fewer than 4,000 tigers remain in the wild—as opposed to perhaps 100,000 at the beginning of the last century.

Yet as these natural populations dwindle, the number of tigers in captivity has soared. Due to the many legal difficulties, the exact population in captivity cannot be known but is thought to range somewhere between 5,000 and 15,000—twice the 4,000 estimated to live in the wild—and most of those are found not in zoos and other commercial enterprises but in the hands of private owners.

Many groups oppose private ownership, from the American Veterinary Medical Association and the Association of Zoos & Aquariums, to the U.S. Department of Agriculture, the Centers for Disease Control and Prevention, and the American Bar Association. Unfortunately, as Professor Nasser points out, the U.S. still has more privately owned tigers than any country.

This is largely due to the inefficiency of existing legislation—the Endangered Species Act and the Animal Welfare Act, among others—which is often stymied by loopholes. Professor Nasser notes that there are such voids that there is no reliable way of even knowing how many captive tigers are in the U.S. The notable technicality is known as the Generic Tiger Loophole in the Endangered Species Act, which, she says, actually incentivizes "captive breeding and exploitation of tigers," and: "the very laws designed to protect and conserve tigers have, in practice, encouraged over-exploitation of tigers for economic gain."

It is Professor Nasser's professional opinion that the existence of the Generic Tiger Loophole in the Endangered Species Act is largely responsible for the vast tiger surplus in the United States. The loophole effectively incentivized entertainers and other unscrupulous breeders to specifically create "generic" tigers in order to evade certain federal agency oversight and permit requirements. Despite the fact that the Generic Tiger Loophole was repealed in 2016, Professor Nasser believes that the impact of the extremely detrimental and misguided regulatory loophole will impact captive tigers for many years to come.

A generic tiger is, by definition, one of an unknown genetic background, or a cross between at least two different subspecies. Because they don't represent any population of tigers found in the wild, they're regarded as having no conservation value by U.S. Fish and Wildlife Service, the America Zoological Association (AZA), and big cat experts. For this reason, the AZA imposed "a breeding moratorium for generic tigers" on all of its member zoos in 2011. Whereas the goal of the AZA's other tiger management programs is to *increase* populations of specific subspecies, the AZA's management program for generic tigers exists for the sole purpose of bringing the population of generic tigers in accredited zoos to zero. What this means is that the only purebred tigers (and thus the only tigers with any conservation value) in America are the few hundred tigers kept in AZA managed breeding programs—but other tigers in America, including all privately-owned tigers are presumptively generic. Stated another way, an estimated ninety-five percent of all captive tigers in the U.S. are generic and lack conservation value.

Professor Nasser takes note of claims by private owners and exhibitors who contend they're "contributing to the valuable conservation of the species." But she doesn't buy it, and neither do most true conservationists. "It is a fiction that most tigers owned by private individuals—such as pet tigers, tigers bred and sold for profit, or white tigers—are valuable for wild conservation," she states in her essay.

It is important to understand, she says, that an estimated ninety percent of wild animals kept as pets die within two years. Moreover, their display and exhibition likely does not help the endangered species, rather it may be "actively detrimental to wild populations of such species." Even the U.S. Fish and Wildlife Service has acknowledged as much.

As the tiger conservationists point out, using them for their entertainment value has led to "the blurring of our awareness of what tigers are and the serious threats wild tigers face to their continued survival," and: "unfettered access to an endangered species lessens public concern for their diminishing numbers in the wild." For as Nasser's colleagues Tilson and Nyhus have said, "People watch the films, they visit the zoos, and by the mesmeric power of these vicarious experiences, they come carelessly to believe that the Bengal tiger...is alive and well because they have seen it."

Or as they bluntly assert: "Genetically indistinguishable alley-cats have no place in realistic conservation."

4

Myths, Facts, and Confusion

You can lead a person to the truth, but you cannot make them think.

The white tiger is a volatile subject surrounded by such misinformation and sleight-of-hand that the beleaguered head of even the most interested person is kept spinning. I call this *convenient confusion*, a ploy instigated by breeders and providers to confuse the average person into believing that inbreeding and the sale of surplus tigers—especially white tigers—are heroic and necessary causes.

My forty-five years of working with dangerous exotic animals has revealed to me how facts can and will be continually twisted to support whatever opinion some person or group wishes to advance. Truth is often a shy voice, and falsehood and inaccuracy are the bullies in the room.

When I speak a truth such as all white tigers in captivity are cross-eyed, the pro-breeding providers immediately argue that white tigers in the wild are normal. While this is in essence true, it's totally irrelevant to my point, which is this: the white tiger, which exists today almost totally in captivity, has been inbred to death. If the original white tiger had been bred scientifically and correctly instead of being treated as an unregulated commercial enterprise, we could have today a white Bengal, genetically pure. There might not be but a handful in captivity, but we would have a valid white Bengal, worthy of saving. Instead, we've created an animal so ecologically useless that it can never be reintroduced into the wild. Or as *Slate* magazine wrote, "Do we really need to be creating more genetic disasters that pull resources away from truly endangered species?"

This redirection of facts causes that *convenient confusion* in the unknowing public.

In the U.S., captive inbreeding of many exotic animals is a popular business. In June of 2011, the board of directors for the America Zoological Association (AZA) formalized a ban on the breeding of white tigers, white lions, or king cheetahs by their member zoos. Their report said in part: "Breeding practices that increase the physical expression of a single rare allele (i.e., rare genetic traits) through intentional breeding, for example intentional breeding to achieve rare color-morphs such as white tigers, deer, and alligators has been clearly linked with various abnormal, debilitating, and at times lethal external and internal conditions and characteristics."

One of the many invaluable resources I was able to draw on for information about white tigers was a veterinarian by the name of Dr. Jennifer Conrad. During near-daily phone calls and texts discussing the plight of the white tiger, Dr. Conrad added to my growing knowledge of the endless health issues suffered by these cats. In addition to those already named, they also have extremely sensitive paws.

Dr. Conrad is internationally known for The Paw Project, her personal crusade to stop the declawing and exploiting of animals. Her mission is to educate the public about the painful and crippling effects of feline declawing and to promote animal welfare through its abolition. She is well known for her surgeries to alleviate the pain for big cats that have been declawed and for rehabilitating them. She said that when white tigers are declawed, their paws become more sensitive, and they also have softer, flaking pads.

The majority of white tigers used in the entertainment field have been declawed. It is done to make them safer to use with celebrities and the public. The older the white tiger gets, the greater the deformity and pain. More weight on surgically altered paws as the big cats grow and mature equals more problems.

Declawing tiger cubs may be great for selfies but a nightmare for adolescent and adult tigers. The paws of these larger declawed big cats will begin to atrophy. Since their claws have been cut out, their paws curl in, and they actually walk on their knuckles. Dr. Conrad says it is like amputating the first knuckles of the fingers of a human. She describes the problem this way: "Think how difficult it would be to pick things up, or tie a shoe. Imagine trying to walk or run if you were a big cat. Tiger's paws sometime flatten out after declawing causing pain when they walk. No claws, no paw control."

A tiger needs its claws to catch prey, maneuver, groom itself, run and play. Declawing a big cat makes it harder to place in sanctuaries. Without their claws, they cannot protect themselves from the other clawed big cats. These big cats will then be a financial burden on any sanctuary that takes them, because they will need further surgeries to keep them mobile and pain free, which are not cheap procedures. Most captive tigers are also kept on concrete to make cleaning easier, which further exacerbates the issue, and the chemicals and constant dampness from cleaning cause the pads to crack and bleed.

A high school student I know went to explore a photo-op tent at our local fair to see what was going on. She decided to get a photo, or so I thought; after all, I saw her approach the line of people waiting their turn. My first response was to be upset, as she knew where I stood on this sort of activity. I thought: *what the heck is she doing?* What happened next changed my anger quickly to a smile.

"Where are this tiger's claws?" she exclaimed as she showed the rest of the crowd what she had observed.

She displayed the clawless cat to the crowd waiting to get their big cat selfies. The crowd was just as shocked as she was, and they felt just as much sympathy for the poor feline as she did. "How is this cub supposed to protect itself? This sucks!" she ranted. When she walked away from the exhibit, she took the majority of people with her. It was brilliant, and the crowd was educated without knowing it was being educated.

Tigers, in general, have soft paw pads that are particularly sensitive to heat—hot sand—or thorny underbrush; the tiger can even sense ground vibrations through its paws. For white tigers, whose already sensitive paws are prone to chafe and shed skin, being declawed quite literally adds injury to insult.

The white tiger faces an impossible standard, as the breeders are seeking perfection. Yet her genetics suggest otherwise. While the white coat is caused by the double recessive gene, most of the cubs born through this inbreeding have normal coloration. And they suffer the same genetic defects. Its worth, however, is predicated upon its coat. Without the white coat, these cubs may be killed at birth because they are considered without value.

They have no conservation purpose, either, because—being a cross between Bengal tigers and Siberian ones—they aren't purebred. What this means is that when the desired coloration or even the proper shade of white does *not* appear—Heaven forbid, if it is born orange—it is discarded like yesterday's trash. In fact, they are referred to as "trash cats."

Dr. Ron Tilson, considered one of the world's leading authorities on tiger conservation, has long pointed out that the white tiger controversy was made of both ethics and economics. The Tiger Species Survival Plan he coordinated condemned the breeding of white tigers "because of their mixed ancestry, most have been hybridized with other subspecies and are of unknown lineage, and because they serve no conservation purpose."

The owners, he noted, saw white tigers as popular in exhibits, and that they increased attendance at zoos, which then increased revenue. "However," he went on to say, "there is an unspoken issue that shames the very integrity of zoos, their alleged 'conservation' programs and their message to visiting public. To produce white tigers or any other phenotypic curiosity, directors of zoos and other facilities must continuously inbreed daughter and father to granddaughter and so on.

"At issue is a contradiction of fundamental genetic principles upon which all species survival plans for endangered species in captivity are based. White tigers are an aberration artificially bred and proliferated by some zoos, private breeders and a few circuses who do so for economic rather than conservation reasons."

Dr. Tilson put the issue even more bluntly: "For private breeders to say we are saving tigers, is a lie. They are not saving tigers, they are breeding them for profit. There are a lot of people doing a lot of terrible things to these animals."

5

Nikki

"Do not take Nikki to that zoo. If they put her in with Ika, he will eat her." —anonymous

Nikki came to me as a newborn surplus tiger cub no longer needed by an AZA zoo in Ohio. She had been part of their "zoo babies" program, and after being passed around to as many paying customers as she could, she became unhealthy and unwanted. This was in the mid-1980s when tiger breeding programs were exploding. Tiger cubs, especially white ones, were the top ticket item for any zoo babies promotions. Those who became not viable enough to show to the public were known as "zoo surplus" and sold off at exotic animal auctions across the country.

One of the largest of these auctions was held four times a year in a little Amish village called Mount Hope, Ohio, about eighty miles north of Columbus. Animal dealers and zoo personnel bring their "surplus" animals from around the U.S. to sell, and the Amish auctioned them off in large barns in the village.

Untrained people could buy venomous snakes, pythons/anacondas, crocodiles/alligators, zebras, giraffes, bears, and big cat cubs by the dozens. No experience necessary, just cash or credit card. They were not illegal, but they were secretive, because the zoos, dealers/breeders, and auctioneers did not want the general public to know this was going on, fearful of being shut down. I know this because I went undercover to film the auctions, and the exposés actually helped stop accredited zoos from selling their unwanted animals. When the public learned zoos were breeding tigers for promotional purposes, then dumping them into these questionable auctions, they were furious.

Nikki was not a healthy cub, and she would have certainly died if she had been sold to an untrained private owner who could not care for her properly. I was worried for Nikki from the moment I fed the poor little girl her first bottle. She was so small and lethargic.

My wife and I took turns feeding her, rubbing her belly and anus with a warm, wet wash rag and letting her snuggle with us for body warmth. We were hoping to imitate the way her mother tiger would feed her, lick her to prevent colic and help the digestive process, and share body contact.

I let Nikki lie on my bare chest so she could hear my heart beat. I had already realized, while raising animals such as wolves, bears, and big cats, that a heartbeat had a soothing effect on the young ones. And so Nikki would relax and fall asleep.

Slowly, she became stronger. She started to walk, growl, and chuff. The larger she got, the more I noticed the white coloration on her back legs and hindquarters. Nikki was definitely not a typical orange tiger, although little did I know that she was a carrier of the white coloration gene. By the time Nikki had reached the age of three, she was already over three hundred pounds, healthy and physically awesome, a far cry from the emaciated cub I had first known.

This was in the mid-1980s, and I was still part of that world of raising cubs and pups. I thought I was rescuing these animals, but later I understood they were not being rescued but were being put back into the breeding cycle of zoos/breeders/dealers. I knew that Nikki now needed to be in a more spacious enclosure than any that I could possibly provide. I put the word out to my acquaintances in the zoo world to find her a new home, and I was immediately contacted by a representative of the Columbus Zoo.

The representative was interested in breeding Nikki with the zoo's male white tiger, Ika, a large three-legged male on loan to the Columbus Zoo from the Hawthorn Corporation, a notorious breeder, dealer, and exhibitor infamous for, among other incidents, its owner being the first person in the country to have an elephant confiscated by the U.S. Department of Agriculture (USDA), after documentation of abuse. A longtime target of PETA (People for the Ethical Treatment of Animals), the Hawthorn Corporation was thought to have caused more pain and suffering for animals, especially tigers, than any other of the known animal exploiters.

Between 2000 and 2011, at least thirty-two tigers owned by the Hawthorn Corporation died from everything from salmonella and renal failure to a faulty cage door, or merely being caged with incompatible tigers who attacked them. Worse, nearly half of them were three years old or younger. What was surprising to me was that at the time Nikki was looking for a new home, the majority of accredited facilities/

circuses were getting their exhibition animals from these horrible animal pimps.

The good news is that the Hawthorn Corporation has since been closed down and the surviving animals relocated. When I learned that Ika was a Hawthorn Corporation tiger, I was hesitant to let Nikki go anywhere near the Columbus Zoo. The plan finally ended when a friend of mine at The Ohio State University Veterinarian School—who was working at the Columbus Zoo—told me," Do not take Nikki to the zoo. If they put her in with Ika, he will eat her!"

My friend also told me that Ika had killed and eaten other female tigers brought to the zoo. I was furious because no one from the zoo had mentioned that Ika was aggressive. I called the zoo representative and wanted to know why no one had told me how dangerous Ika was, and the rep kept telling me what I had heard was all just vicious rumor and I should believe him.

I did not tell him where I got my information, or from whom. I hung up and tried to calm down. Nikki had trusted me, and I had almost sent her to be killed. I needed to tread more carefully in checking out potential facilities. Nikki had a sweet temperament that I knew would change when she turned five years old. She might still chuff and rub, but she could not stop her instincts, and she could kill me just by playing rough.

Weeks went by as I checked and double-checked accredited facilities. I investigated and spoke with people that worked in any way with, or were close to, each facility. Finally, I found an accredited zoo in a nearby state that worked out perfectly.

I didn't see Nikki again for eight years. When I finally went back to pay her a visit, I stood with the other zoo visitors looking over the rail, surrounded by about thirty people, kids, and adults. As I watched the two tigers walking in their enclosure, I immediately recognized her. A smile came over my face. She seemed so relaxed and she looked beautiful.

Just as I started to blend into the crowd, I heard a growling roar, followed by loud chuffing and whining. I pushed back through the crowd and was stunned to see Nikki standing as close as she could to the moat, calling out.

I thought, *She could not have recognized me; it's been eight years.* But as I approached the rail, Nikki became excited, pacing back and forth, side-to-side. She was whining and chuffing at me. I wanted to make sure, so I walked in front of all the people along the rail. And Nikki followed me, prancing and whining. She remembered me.

My emotions ran from being happy to being sad that I couldn't go near her. I also felt what a shame that a beautiful, healthy tiger had to live her life, not in the wilds of Nepal or India, but in an enclosure. Both my mind and my feelings were racing and my heart was pounding out of my chest.

Then the people standing at the railing started to realize Nikki was talking to *me*. I was suddenly rushed by thirty-plus strangers wanting to know why this tiger appeared to be in love with me. I just walked away.

Seeing Nikki triggered emotions in me that caught me entirely by surprise. And while the scientists still debate if attributing emotions to animals can explain aspects of their behavior that reward-and-threat mechanisms don't cover, she clearly recognized me, which loaded on my guilt for "giving" her away. What was she "thinking" when I turned away from her? I was as overwhelmed with the same painful emotions I had the first time I left her.

I would *never* own a big cat again. I realized I could only help these big cats by rescuing them and working with facilities that want to make a real place for captive big cats to retire with respect.

I walked away, never to go back again.

6
CONservation

It's totally a con. Let's just call it CONservation.

Siegfried and Roy preached about their magnificent Royal White tigers. Yet the title—"Royal White"—was nothing more than a made-up marketing gimmick two magicians used to sell themselves. They were so clever they actually marketed what they were doing as *conservation*. And that may have been Siegfried and Roy's most accomplished illusion.

The misrepresentation of these big cats suckered a naïve public into believing that by using these exploited animals in a magic show, they were saving the wild tigers in India. Or that the white tigers were a separate species that had to be saved. Stop and think for a second: by using the so-called "Royal White" tigers in a magic act, the public becomes educated about the wild tiger's behavior and environment?

Wild tiger *behavior*?

Jumping through flaming hoops and walking on a leash in front of hundreds of clapping people—four shows a day! Are we expected to believe that this is tiger behavior in the wild? How about environment? These tigers live in transport cages and spend most of their days doing live magic shows.

Sometimes, Roy would get them out of their cages to swim in his pool for photo opportunities. This is the environment wild tigers live in? This misrepresentation of the white tiger was extremely lucrative for Siegfried and Roy: the white tigers catapulted their shows into sold-out performances, with ticket prices escalating and hard to get.

Siegfried and Roy began breeding their "Royal White" tigers, using the cubs as props for media blasts and advertising. Celebrities and VIP customers were lining up to get their picture taken with these newborn cubs, whose eyes were barely open. The exploitation of these cubs is why I call these types of exploiters "animal pimps."

If Siegfried and Roy really cared about these cubs, they would not endanger the newly born animals by having them interact with the public. The stress alone is health threatening. But the magicians needed these props for their continued success selling tickets—not for the safety of their white tigers and certainly not for tigers in the wild.

⌒

Siegfried and Roy became the number one breeders of the "Royal White" tigers in the U.S.—not an accredited zoo or conservation organization but two magicians doing a Las Vegas magic act. Does anyone else see the problem with this scenario? Do you think the breeding was scientifically done? Do you think there wasn't any interbreeding with birth defects? There is nothing about the "Royal White" tiger's experience in the U.S. that has been royal. Paraded about as "ambassadors" and "royal" was a grand irony, for they never were treated in such a manner.

And so began the influx of white tigers sold to the general public, from a million-dollar home in Las Vegas to backyards across the country. Within a few years, white tigers were appearing everywhere: roadside zoos, basements, backyards, and in the company of entertainers. The explosion of private breeders caused even more of a surplus of white tigers.

As Siegfried and Roy's popularity grew exponentially with that of the "Royal Whites," a new term was added to the world of animal exploitation—"'designer' big cats." These tigers became stylish because of Siegfried and Roy and vice versa. The average person paid big bucks for a ticket to see their show but never got the message of conservation from the patter of these popular magicians.

In fact, it was just the opposite. When asked what message they got from the Siegfried and Roy act, people invariably said, "I want a white tiger as a pet." Somewhere, the message of conservation got lost among all the magic tricks, flashing lights, and explosions. Models, celebrities, and politicians demanded to be photographed with a white tiger cub.

The celebrities, VIP customers, and photo-op patrons never think where these cubs come from, or where they went after their encounter. Unfortunately, they only care that they have their own personal experience with a white tiger. They care about the photo they will be showing off on Facebook and Instagram. They think of only themselves and their short time with the ultimate designer animal.

We have all seen designer animals. They are the ones used in product advertisements. The black leopard walking with the model, or the tiger being used to promote a TV series or sporting event. These animals are supplied by animal entertainment companies. Over the years, I have been observing this virtual explosion of imagery in which white tigers, usually cubs, are seen on everything from posters, puzzles, t-shirts/sweaters, and calendars to television shows, photo ops at fairs, malls, festivals, and birthday parties. Millions of dollars have been made by the exploitation of white tigers.

Many people who adopt a white tiger (from an alleged 'conservation' organization) do so only with the best of intentions, wishing to save tigers in the wild. If these good-hearted people actually knew where the majority of the money ended up, they would be appalled.

I am still trying to figure out how adopting a white tiger in the U.S. has any conservation or educational connection to wild tigers. This is totally a con. So let's just call it *CONservation*.

Now we have learned how the white tiger was introduced to the U.S. The Cincinnati Zoo sold a pair of white tigers to two magicians in Las Vegas. The magicians made money by exploiting and over-breeding them, and the cubs that couldn't be used ended up with private breeders across the country.

The misuse by private, untrained breeders caused the horrible inbreeding and physical handicaps we have seen over the last twenty years. Private breeding has saturated the market with white tigers. They are found everywhere, and I have personally removed them from corn cribs, barns, and basements. Every zoo, roadside zoo, circus, magic act, traveling photo op, and exploitative entertainment company has these animals. The white tiger is now firmly entrenched as a part of America's culture.

The story that I think emphasizes the white tiger's dilemma in America is the story of Montecore, the white tiger that attacked Roy on stage during one of the Siegfried and Roy Vegas performances. Afterward, the experts and pontificators debated what made the tiger "turn on" Roy, but to my mind, the only person who got it right was the American comedian Chris Rock.

Rock performed an equally hilarious and insightful stand-up routine (now found on *YouTube*, see: "Chris Rock Tiger Gone Crazy") in which he postulated that contrary to what the experts were saying Montecore didn't go *crazy* but, "That tiger went tiger."

I agree whole-heartedly with this assessment. That tiger didn't do anything other than precisely what a tiger is supposed to do. The only time the tiger wasn't doing what it was supposed to be doing was—as Chris Rock put it "...when the tiger was ridin' around on a little bike with a Hitler helmet on."

Tigers are not supposed to jump through hoops or do magic tricks. They are supposed to kill. Tigers are the world's largest predatory cat, a perfect killing machine. Where does it ever say a tiger should be doing magic tricks in Las Vegas?

White tigers would continually pop up in my life. I fell for the propaganda that white tigers were an endangered species and must be bred in captivity to save the wild Bengal tigers. As everyone else in the 1960s and 1970s, we believed the exploitation of these white tiger cubs by accredited zoos and conservation educators was just part of protecting the wild tigers. It was how education was done.

This exploitation of wildlife began in the 1940s with Frank Buck of *Bring 'em Back Alive* fame. Frank would go with his team into wild areas of the world and capture tiger cubs and other animals for zoos. Sometimes he killed the mother animals in order to take their young, all in the name of science and education. His movies and newsreels were brutal. Harassing and teasing animals to get them to be aggressive makes the visuals more exciting for the viewers, even as many of his scenes were staged.

This style of film-making continued with Marlin Perkins and Jim Fowler's *Mutual of Omaha's Wild Kingdom* television show, the Man-versus-Nature style that we all thought was helping animals in the wild. While we thought these "Animal Ambassadors" were maybe roughed around a little, surely they were treated with care afterward. This "Animal Ambassador" gimmick continued with Jack Hanna, Steve Irwin, Dave Salmoni, and many other animal entertainment "stars."

Once the white tigers made their grand entrance on American shores, they became poster children. The most famous of all the "Animal Ambassadors," white tiger cubs were popping up everywhere. Television talk shows were constantly displaying a crying, stressed cub with a TV animal educator, passing it around to all the celebrities on the show. The audiences clapped and shouted as the lights and cameras were forced in the young cubs' faces.

Tigers—and all big cats—have extremely sensitive hearing, eyesight, and sense of smell. (Their hearing is so acute they can hear their prey from a mile away, and Indonesian hunters were said to carefully barber themselves because they believed a tiger could hear "the wind whistling through a man's nose hairs.")

This overstimulation of their senses causes stress and health issues, both physically and mentally. White tigers have poor vision and many difficult physical and mental disabilities caused by years of interbreeding. Using them as "ambassadors" is cruel.

I did not know this in the 1960s, 1970s, and the early 1980s. I believed what the 'conservation experts' were saying. I thought white tiger cubs were needed for educational conservation purposes. This is what we were led to believe by Frank, Marlin, Jack, and David, as well as our zoos and learning institutes. This naïveté came to a screeching halt the first time I was called out to rescue and relocate a tiger from a basement. I was shocked and had my baptism in reality.

The tiger was in a basement in Cincinnati's Over-the-Rhine neighborhood, and the tiger was *white*. I couldn't believe what I was seeing. The 'conservationists' had been telling me it was so rare that there was no private ownership of it. There was no way anyone had a white tiger as a *pet*. They existed only in *zoos*. Yet here it was, in front of me. In a *basement*.

I immediately called Jack Hanna. He was my hero, the figurehead of the conservationists, and I still wanted to believe him. No, he said. There were no white tigers as pets. But how else would this tiger have gotten into an Over-the-Rhine basement? It was like I'd stumbled across Bigfoot. It took some time, maybe a month or two, but it was my epiphany: I was being lied to.

All these so-called conservationists were lying.

7

Cats, Celebrities, and Cops

Please, do not believe a word I have told you. Go out and investigate it yourself. You will find it is worse than what I have told you.

As a result of the examples I have detailed, my world of wildlife heroes came crashing down. I realized I was supporting a belief that was not only false but cruel. I was promoting this culture and so I was part of the problem, not the solution. I had to stand up and tell anyone who would listen what was really going on. The people I thought were my friends and family immediately turned on me. And my life changed.

I began asking myself questions I would never previously have even dreamed that I would. How did a white tiger end up in a backyard in Ohio? How did a white tiger from the Maharaja of Rewa (Mohini) begin the mass breeding from zoos, backyards, and private dealers across the country? How can a private owner buy a white tiger?

Those were just a few questions I had. My understanding was that white tigers were an endangered species. This was common knowledge. Little did I know, however, that white tigers had become a major commodity. The white tiger had become the "it" animal. Hundreds of white cubs were born, even as hundreds more were rejected because of their orange color. This hunger for white tiger cubs became insatiable.

The demand by zoos and TV wildlife educators flooded the market with cubs (both white and orange). Millions of dollars were made by any zoo that had a white tiger cub. Zoos realized they could use the white cubs for photos, keep some as they got older to pull in visitors, and sell many more at substantial prices to private breeders. From the 1960s through the 1980s you could see white tiger cubs in the "zoo babies" programs, but by the next year they had disappeared. You could see zoo babies but no zoo teenagers.

As I began to attend exotic animal auctions and check classified ads in newspapers, I discovered that these zoo babies ended up auctioned and sold to the highest bidder. The majority of people buying them had no idea how to care for—or raise—a tiger safely.

In 1981, I was hired by the City of Oakwood Public Safety Department to be trained as a police officer/firefighter/EMT-paramedic. Prior to joining the force, in my capacity as a veterinary technician, I had responded for years to help law enforcement, fire departments, and animal control officials with dangerous exotic/wild animal dispatches. Now that I was a public safety officer, I was amazed at how many of my fellow officers recounted incidents with big cats.

This really opened my eyes to the problem. At that time, I was taking rescued wild/exotic animals on a national TV show called *The Daily Buzz*. I was doing what the other

TV wildlife hosts were doing, but mine were actual rescues off the streets and out of homes in the tristate area (Ohio, Indiana, and Kentucky). I thought I was doing the right thing, educating through entertainment.

Yeah, maybe the animals were stressed, but it was for the betterment of their species—right? I was telling myself the same lies that 'conservationists' probably tell themselves so they can sleep at night.

On one of my appearances with *The Daily Buzz*, I showed up with a six-month old tiger cub. It was walking down Main Street in Dayton, Ohio, a pet that had gotten loose, and the Dayton police were ready to shoot it. Recognizing it as a cub, I pulled up in my cruiser, opened the back door, and called to it. Tired and thirsty, it saw the back seat of my cruiser as a haven, jumped in, and away we drove.

Before I found a sanctuary for it, reality again smacked me in my face. I always let the TV show crews bring their family and friends to the show to meet my animal guest, and when the show finished, I walked the tiger off the set to meet them.

As everyone lined up for photos, I had a sudden revelation. So I began asking the kids questions about tigers. "Where are tigers supposed to live?" I asked. None of the children were sure what countries tigers even came from. Most of the children—and adults, as well—just said they wanted to get a tiger cub. It was exactly the opposite of my intended message, which I had intended to be one of conservation and leaving the animals in the wild.

Apparently, no one had been listening. They had only seen the tiger and me handling it. *They* wanted to be the one handling the tiger. They all wanted to either own a tiger or have their photo taken with a tiger. This reality check changed the way I was going to have to present my message. I was going to have to speak on TV shows without dragging an animal out to be exhibited as an *ambassador*. How was I going to educate the public about tigers without actually bringing one?

It hadn't been done on TV. I was told by all the top animal educators—Jack Hanna, Jeff Corwin, Dave Salmoni, and Jarod Miller—it could *never* be done. But for the tiger's sake, I would have to break this medieval practice. I would have to actually care about the tiger cubs instead of simply using them as props.

This would prove to be a novel undertaking. As I quickly found out, it would also ostracize me from the mainstream animal and conservation experts. Apparently, the unorthodox methodology of actually caring for tiger cubs was a new concept. Deep down, of course, I should have known. After all, we know how history treats people who buck the system. Because I worked as a police officer, I was used to verbal and psychological abuse from the public. This harassment training made me the perfect person to stand up for tiger cubs. As a result of what I have experienced over the years, particularly in actually trying to protect animals, I always tease that I have only one feeling left, which I have saved for my wife.

Little did I know that this seemingly common-sense approach—refusing to abuse tigers for entertainment—would actually cripple my ability to get donations, and it almost shut down my non-profit. No tiger cub to display, no donations. No tiger cub to display, no speaking engagements. No tiger cub to display, no organization to save them. What a catch-22: to acquire money to protect and save tigers, I needed to breed and harass tigers.

No one knew what happened to tiger cubs when they grew too large to be used for VIP parties and photo opportunities. They seemed to disappear into the auction world and become either private pets, used in canned hunts, or sold for body parts. Whatever you do, do not ask animal educators what actually happened to that cute white tiger cub they were using as an ambassador animal on the TV talk shows. That line of questioning will cause blank looks, aggressive verbal attacks, and an overall "I-don't-care-what-happened-to-them" type of response. (Little did I know that I was going to have to protect the cats from the world-famous experts as well.)

It is nice for our animal heroes to lecture us on saving the tigers in the wild, but who is going to save the tiger cub sitting in their laps on *Jimmy Kimmel Live*? These tiger cubs are the tigers that are most in danger.

Go to India or Nepal and the researchers can tell you where the majority of tigers are located in the wild. They've tagged them with tracking devices. In the U.S., when a tiger cub goes on TV and hits the talk show circuit, VIP parties, and photos ops, and then is dumped when it becomes too large and dangerous, there is no such system in place to track it.

I have begged for years to have all tigers and big cats micro-chipped or tattooed so we can follow where they go. But this practice of protecting big cats has been shut down by the self-same animal 'conservationists.' The reason is simple: as long as the animals cannot be tracked, the TV animal hosts and photo op groups can continue to have tigers bred unchecked. They could keep getting fresh cubs each year, breeding more young ones and dumping the old ones without anyone from the public knowing what had happened to them. Hypocrisy is too casual a word to describe this practice.

When asked, the TV animal host and private breeders could say without fear of correction, "It is not against the law." Now you see why they fight so hard to keep regulations and laws from being passed. I say, "Just because you can do it, doesn't mean it's right." It is not the cub's fault it is here, but it is *our* fault if we don't help them.

Next time you watch your favorite late night TV show, ask yourself, "What is going to happen to that cute little white tiger cub after the show?" Then do your own investigation. When I speak at universities, high schools, and elementary schools, I always finish my lectures with the words, "Please do not believe a word I have told you. Go out and investigate it yourself. You will find out it is worse than what I have told you."

―――

White tigers were quite the novelty in the late 1950s to 1970s. The National Zoo in Washington, DC, and the Cincinnati Zoo in Ohio were the original places to see a white tiger in the USA. Because I lived near Cincinnati and grew up in that era, I went to the Cincinnati Zoo with my family and on school field trips. I vividly remember the original white tigers. I was intrigued by the unique coloration of their fur and their stunning blue eyes.

I have blue eyes, and I thought how cool that these big cats and I had something in common. My cousins and I bought T-shirts with tiger images on them. Friends and family would tease me and call me "White Tiger." It became my favorite big cat.

I listened to the zoo educators telling groups of tourists how these beautiful animals are a special breed of Bengal tiger—extremely rare and endangered in the wild. We were told that the breeding of these big cats was very important for the endangered orange tigers in the wilds of Nepal and India. The white tigers in captivity will save the wild tigers by being ambassador animals.

I believed them (at first), especially because they were educators and guides trained by the Cincinnati Zoo. This is when I was introduced to the *ambassador animal* style of drawing people to a zoo or TV show. The textbook definition is something like that expressed by *The Mother Nature Network*, which says, "For young children and adults alike, the thrill of being close to a wild animal can spark a lifelong interest in learning more about a species or ecosystem, and importantly, in environmental conservation. So ambassador animals are some of the most important members of their species."

Nothing wrong with *that*, right? But when we look at the white tiger, the real truth behind the term "ambassador animal" is quite different. What it really means is that an educational conservation group, such as a zoo or animal TV host, takes a tiger cub away from its mother to be *hand-raised*. The "experts" say they have to remove the cub because the mother does not know how to care for it or was threatening to kill it. The "experts" say they are protecting the cub. (Says one animal rescuer, "News stories always quote the zoo owners saying such nonsense.")

Even though I was in elementary school when I first heard this concept, I knew it was bogus. Why would a species of big cats lose its natural instinct to care for their cubs? How could literally hundreds of tiger cubs be born yearly for just educational purposes? Did all these female tigers suddenly and conveniently lose their mothering capabilities?

When I raised my hand at the tours and asked, "Do any of these tigers go back to the wild?" the answer was always, "No, but in the near future we'll be releasing them back into the wild." I would then ask, "Why are you breeding so many, and where do they go when they get too big?"

Other people on the tours would turn and look at me, wondering the same thing. The zoo guide would simply cut me off with a cryptic response, "We trade them to other accredited zoos. Next question."

Every year I went to the Cincinnati Zoo and saw only a few tigers, I asked myself the same questions. Being a young kid, I didn't have the power or the resources to try and find out the truth about where these tiger cubs, both white and orange, might end up. As I grew older and was able to actually gather those resources, I found out and, sadly, almost wished I hadn't.

Not only did I find out how tigers like these were disposed of, I also learned that no captive tiger raised in an accredited zoo in North America has *ever* been released back into the wilds of Nepal or India. That has not stopped the breeding in the U.S., though. It has not stopped the use of ambassador animals on TV entertainment shows. It has not stopped the use of tiger cubs for photo opportunities at zoos, fairs, birthday parties, malls, weddings, and TV commercials. And it has definitely not stopped the poaching of endangered tigers in the wild. Wasn't that what the breeding and exploitation was for? It has made millions for zoos, private breeders, magicians, animal TV 'conservationists,' and TV wildlife producers, but at what cost?

The biggest big cat mystery of our times has always been: what happened to the white tiger cubs seen sitting in David Letterman's lap after they were carried backstage. Where did they go when they were no longer needed? As I grew older, this nagging question haunted me. What made me mad was that no one could (or would) tell me. The cubs just seemed to disappear. And by my own rough estimate, there were probably thousands of them.

It made no sense to me; an alleged endangered species could not be located? If this were Nepal or India, it would have been an international wildlife crime. In the U.S., no one seemed to even question the beloved TV animal hosts. The average viewer was (and is still) led to believe that the white tigers just went back to an accredited zoo. When Jack Hanna was passing around white tiger cubs, we thought they were from the Columbus Zoo. After all, that is what we were told. We thought that when all the celebrities finished holding the stressed cubs, they went back to some beautiful spacious facility fit for an *ambassador*. Jack even said in one of the shows that some of the big cats live in "a thousand-acre facility."

When I started to investigate, I discovered that most of the big cats (Amur leopards, snow leopards, African lions, cougars, and African leopards) were *not*, in fact, from the Columbus Zoo. They were bred by private breeders or other non-AZA facilities. These white tiger cubs were born in puppy mills for endangered cats. When I finally was able to ask Jack, David, Jarod, and the other animal "conservationists" about the big cat cubs they used on their television shows, VIP parties, and photo opportunities, their original response was: "They go to nice accredited zoos."

When I investigated this claim, I found that the cubs were not from *any* AZA zoos. AZA facilities do not allow endangered big cat cubs to be used for entertainment and exploitation. On further investigation, I discovered that the cubs seemed to mysteriously disappear after doing the TV shows and VIP party circuit. When their use was over, they were whisked away by mysterious "providers." What the heck is a "provider?"

I learned the term "provider" was used by all the animal entertainment experts. A provider is a private, non-accredited supplier that is contacted to find a white tiger cub to be used and then made to disappear afterwards. This shocked even me, and I thought I had seen everything. Many of these cubs were from backyards of private breeders, unregulated and without compassion.

To these breeders, selling a tiger cub is no different from selling a lawnmower. The difference is that when you are done with your lawnmower you can put it in the garage. A tiger is much more difficult to put away after its use. Every year, I see new tiger cubs born into this world. For years, Siegfried and Roy used the births of hundreds of tiger cubs as an international publicity stunt. Many of the cubs were white tigers. The media, as well as paying customers, fell all over themselves to have their photos taken with these beautiful animals.

When that batch of cubs grew too large and dangerous to exploit, what happened to them? Count the cubs exploited from just the last twenty-five years, then count how many you see at the magic shows or zoos, and then ask yourself: where are the surplus cubs?

I started out simply. I went to the Columbus Zoo looking for the white tiger cubs I had just seen on *Late Night with David Letterman*. They were not there, and they were not going to be there. As just one example, a *YouTube* video showed Jack Hanna on one of his many appearances on *David Letterman*, and he mentioned the cats came from the Columbus Zoo.

I would ask zoo employees where the cubs were and they responded, "They do not stay at the Columbus Zoo." When I pushed for a more solid answer, I would get a blank stare and they would walk away. I decided to investigate the mystery myself.

Any good law enforcement officer would start an investigation by contacting the last person seen with the victim. I decided to ask for help from the animal conservation heroes. They would immediately step up to help find these missing cubs, right?

But when I tried to contact major players in the animal entertainment business, no one responded. I sent dozens of emails, made phone calls and personal visits to zoo officials. Nothing worked. As a cop, I knew that since these attempts didn't work, I had to find them at their homes or personal appearances. I had to go face-to-face. When I tracked them down, asking about specific cats by name, I still got no satisfactory answer. The stone walls had grown even higher and thicker.

Then one day, I asked about a specific cat by the name of Yuki.

8

Yuki

Where is Yuki?

Yuki was a white cub who vanished from the entertainment circuit, and when I began to ask the 'conservationists' who'd displayed her, they said they didn't know where she was. Yuki and a sibling had both disappeared, and the 'conservationists' said the cubs had been brought to them by "providers," they'd seen them for only a short period of time, and afterward they had no idea where they went.

I told them all that I was going to do an investigation much like a police officer does for missing children. I talked to these 'entertainment conservationists' one by one, looked them in the eye, and said, "I have to start with you. You were the last person seen with the cubs." Their nonchalant attitude reflected back to me was maddening. I have helped rescue, relocate, and care for over a hundred big cats. I can tell you where every one of them is currently located. If someone approached me and said they couldn't find one of the big cats I worked with, I would first be stunned, then I'd stop immediately and make sure the big cat was safe. I would drop everything to find the big cat.

These attitudes stoked me to put a team together to find at least some of these missing animals. Because the "experts" appeared unconcerned, we had to step up and do what major animal conservation groups, both good and bad, said couldn't be done. Finding people to help was not hard. I quickly found volunteers: law enforcement officers, a federal wildlife investigator, a big cat private investigator, an attorney, an investigative journalist, and some exceptional Michigan State law students.

David Salmoni, of *Discovery Channel/Animal Planet* fame, actually looked me in the eye and said, "It's very unlikely anyone's gonna help you with this." This after I begged him to help me find the Ambassador big cat cubs he had used on TV promotions. David said, "There is no upside to telling you or helping you in any way." David could have just punched me in the face and it would have had the same effect.

Now I had to find out. The lives of nearly hundreds of big cat cubs and Ambassador animals were at stake. I asked David if the cubs he used just disappear and he responded, "If you can't find them, it doesn't mean they disappeared. It means you need to learn how to find them better." And so we did.

The investigators helping me continued to search for the vanishing Ambassador big cat cubs, and the public may be surprised to learn where some of these high-profile endangered species were dumped. There were two leopards that the owner of a backyard, non-accredited privately-owned "zoo" called, Critter Country Farm, (hidden in the hills of Pennsylvania) stated were used by David Salmoni as Ambassador cubs on national TV shows.

During my investigation, I found that nine tiger cubs were leased to Massillon High school in Ohio for their Obie mascot program. These tiger cubs would be dragged growling and crying from one public event to another until the big football game. At the football game, there are thousands of screaming fans, helicopters, fireworks, and gawkers traumatizing the young cub. These tiger cubs vanish after their use was done. These cubs were leased from Cindy Huntzman of the questionable non-accredited backyard menagerie, Stump Hill Farms. Cindy was also well known as the supplier of Ambassador animals for Jack Hanna, America's Best-Loved Conservationist...WOW! (Cleveland 19-"Official Wants to Keep Track of Tiger Mascots")

Our investigation led us to another backyard menagerie not known or open to the public in the outback of Pennsylvania. This place had numerous makeshift cages and clutter everywhere. Definitely not a facility to get or place endangered big cats. This place also was a supplier of big cat cubs for a price for entertainment purposes. This man was one of the "go-to guys" for animal exploitation. I personally talked to him and he said he had big cats, but he still keeps the ones used by popular TV animal conservationists. He never dumps them anywhere else. As the investigation continued, we found that was not a true statement.

The white tiger cub is seen with animal conservationist, Jarod Miller on the TV show, *Regis and Kelly*, is a perfect match to the white tiger cub seen with a private owner, Andrew Simmons, at his own home. Their stripes, like fingerprints, line up perfectly. Andrew Simmons was frequently seen handling big cat cubs with Jarod Miller on national TV morning shows. When I asked Jarod about that white tiger cub he acted dumbfounded and could not remember this cub, there have been so many, he is only around them for fifteen minutes for the shows. He said the same thing all the other animal conservationists have told me, "I don't know."

I was saddened to discover that many of the white tiger cubs died during transport to be used as Ambassador cubs. Some even died after continually being brought out to be handled and passed around on TV shows and personal appearances. The constant stress on an infant animal bouncing around the country in vans and sleeping in dog carriers at hotels can kill these sensitive animals. These providers, private breeders, and popular animal 'conservationists' are breeding strictly for the purposes of exploitation, caring nothing at all about the high mortality rate of over-breeding and transporting infant cubs for pay-to-play situations. The cubs are a commodity. Their deaths, or the dumping of them in backyards and non-accredited facilities, is merely business as usual.

We always do our homework before I speak to these 'conservationists'. I know the answer to my questions before I ask them. This is an old police investigation technique that will prove if the subject is telling the truth or lying. Andrew was definitely the "provider" for Jarod on *Regis and Kelly*; you can see him bring the cub out and take it away. What is even more incriminating is that the white tiger cub then appears as a promotional tool on his website posing and playing on what appears to be Andrew's kitchen table. "I don't know" does not cut it as a response. As it was with

Yuki, this white tiger cub apparently disappeared, and no one seen with her seemed to care.

I know this is true because I asked them myself. Straight from the horse's mouth. Jack Hanna, Jarod Miller, and the rest of these 'conservationists' are the guiltiest of this hypocrisy. They are educated and believed to be the most trusted animal educators on the planet. And while they should know this manipulation of animals is wrong, they still appear to allow and support this behavior, which anyone with common sense would agree is wrong.

Jack Hanna has battled us everywhere we tried to get legislation or regulations passed for the protection of big cats. Suzi Rapp, Jack's and the Columbus Zoo's big cat expert, when asked by me why she and Jack could not support the Big Cat Public Safety Act (now in the House of Representatives for a vote) stated, "That Law shuts us down." That statement says it all. Jack and Suzi could not do business as usual if they could not get these Ambassador animals.

Yuki's story struck me hard. Yuki was a white tiger cub that was being used for animal entertainment by a close acquaintance of Jack Hanna, Jungle Joe Fortunato. Jungle Joe had a traveling educational animal show and acquired Yuki to be used for his appearances and promotions.

Jack Hanna supported Jungle Joe's mission. Jack also posed with Jungle Joe for promotional photos that were all over the Jungle Joe's Wildlife Adventures site. Some people remember Jungle Joe from his now-defunct Buck County Zoo, or his many TV appearances on shows like the *Today Show, The Meredith Vieira Show*, the *CBS Early Show* as well as being seen with the Kratt Brothers for photos with animals.

During our investigation, I had an informant that worked for Jungle Joe Fortunato that stated after Joe was done with Yuki, that cub was hard to place. My informant had no idea what happened to Yuki. There was another white tiger cub at the Jungle Joe's warehouse named Larka, but Jungle Joe promoted her under the name, Snow-White. The informant believed that white tiger cub died from an E. coli infection. If Yuki was caged in that warehouse with poor ventilation and no sunlight, Yuki could have also contracted E. coli and may have died. If Yuki was sickly when Jungle Joe tried to dump her, this could explain why she was so hard to place. White tiger cubs are like gold, it would not be hard to place a healthy one. This is the warehouse Jack Hanna supported and was quoted in the local newspaper *The Reporter*, "Pass the word around and support this place." This makes what happened to Yuki a bigger mystery. If this is what happens to endangered big cats in the USA, our popular 'conservationists' are no different than the poachers in India. The difference is the poachers may not know what they are doing is wrong, but these 'conservationists' certainly should.

Then she disappeared, and no one seemed to know what happened to her. But I thought Joe and Jack could likely tell me. I thought this would be a simple task. I first tried to call them, then I emailed them, but I received no response from either of them.

Some people may think they are not obligated to speak to me. For those, I submit the following arguments: First, I am no stranger to them. Technically, aren't we all supposed to be on the same team? Second, even if they didn't know me personally, the documentary *The Elephant in the Living Room* exposed people to the sinister world of animal exploitation, and I am sure they are familiar with it. Last, it's simply the right thing for them to do. If they're not hiding anything, shouldn't these 'animal conservationists' care enough about Yuki to contact me and ask how to help?

After months without any response, I decided to go face to face with Yuki's alleged caretakers. With the team of investigators on my side, we were able to find where Jungle Joe lived. As I approached his residence, I had my list of big cat cubs, complete with names, biographical data, and photos in hand.

Yuki was number one, page one. I looked at her face and a feeling of rage pushed aside all other emotions. How dare these people abuse a beautiful creature like her? The idea of invading Joe's privacy didn't bother me anymore. When I remembered the hundreds of cats whose privacy and homes and actual freedom had been stolen from them by these men for years, that was all that mattered. Where the hell was Yuki? What did they do to her?

Then my old cop mentality checked in and calmed me down so I could do my job without completely losing my temper. As I approached the door, I knew exactly what I needed to do. I knocked on the door, it opened, and there in front of me was Jungle Joe Fortunato wearing a dark Krav Maga martial arts shirt. He asked me what I wanted. I politely asked him if he would like to go down the street to a coffee shop or restaurant so we could discuss things in private. I did not want to embarrass him right in front of his family. He said he didn't want to, and he asked me again what I wanted.

Even though he knew who I was, I gave him my name and told him I had been trying to contact him. I showed him the list of big cat cubs with the photo of Yuki staring out from the front page. His face went taut and his cheeks turned red. I then asked him bluntly, "Where is Yuki?"

He said he didn't know and that he'd lost all his records. He said he had over eighty-seven animals and couldn't remember all of them.

"This was the only white tiger cub you had," I said, "and you used her all over your promotion photos. It is impossible for you not to remember." He began a tale of woe about people coming after him "unjustly."

I interrupted him and said, "I don't care about you; where is Yuki?" The victim in this case certainly wasn't him.

Then he stammered about an accredited AZA zoo where the cats would go afterward. How infuriating it was. He described his interactions with the innocent cats as "when I was done using them." I asked him to tell me the names of any accredited facilities where he had supposedly sent the cats. Jungle Joe looked at me with a stunned gaze and told me again, "I lost the records."

At this point I asked him, "Are you going to help me find Yuki?" He circled back to the common response I seemed to get from all these 'conservation educators.' "No," he said, "and I don't have to tell you."

As I walked away I was suddenly stopped in my tracks. Emotionally, I felt I was going to explode. Here is a guy who could help me stop the abuse of big cat cubs and help me find Yuki. Here is a 'conservationist' and educator looking me in the face and lying to me. As a law enforcement officer, I know that the only people who lie to me are bad guys. Crazy thing about Jungle Joe Fortunato is that he, too, is a law enforcement officer.

Periodically, I survey people who have just visited the Columbus Zoo. I ask them about watching Jack on *David Letterman* and other TV shows. Although the faces have changed, the answers—sadly—have remained the same. They seem intrigued and many of them say they'd like to own one.

All they see is a cute tiger cub, and they want one. Any time I speak to the public about where they think these white tigers came from, they seem convinced they come from the Columbus Zoo. If I then ask where they think the rare cubs go after the TV show, they all respond, the Columbus Zoo.

But then I ask them, "Did you see the white tigers in the zoo today?" Some answer that they had not. Some walked away. Some, however, pay attention and respond by saying, "That is a good question. I'm going to have to find out." I invite them all to join my quest to find the many white tiger cubs that have been used by Jack.

But of all the white tiger cubs we have searched for, we have not been able to find Yuki. Some of our informants think she died soon after her promotional use was over. White tiger cubs do have a history of inbred defects, and many die at a young age from birth defects and other ailments. But no evidence of a white tiger cub matching Yuki's facial stripes—a tiger's facial stripes are like the fingerprints of a human; no two are the same—was found by any zoo or sanctuary, which gives me probable cause to believe Yuki never made it out of that warehouse in Pennsylvania. Yuki's story is not surprising, but it is a wake-up call to any who truly care about white tigers.

9

Nikita and Nora

Victims of the curse.

Many people believe that all tigers are created equal. They seem to think tigers have the same personalities. I can say without question: this is a myth. All cats have distinct personalities, whether it's your domestic house cat or a white tiger. To illustrate my point, I am going to introduce you to two white tigers.

Nikita, an aggressive, violently explosive white tiger, came from a horribly abusive background. She was rumored to have grabbed a man by the throat, injuring him severely. She was constantly on edge, snarling, growling, and erupting every time someone walked past her cage.

She showed symptoms of mental trauma, like that of an abused child. I know this from my experience as a police officer. I was trained to identify behavior that signaled an abused victim, and taking this training and applying it to tigers, it is easy to diagnose Nikita's obvious mental status.

Nikita is the yin of the yin-yang symbol, the former representing hate, dark, negative, and death in the Chinese culture. The yang—positive, light, birth—is Nora. Nora came from the same environment as Nikita and was possibly more abused than Nikita. Yet Nora never showed any signs of aggression. She would chuff and rub against her cage, always happy and in good spirits. When a tiger chuffs, they are comfortable and appear happy. It is a calming noise made through their mouth and nose, one of nature's most beautiful sounds. It is your house cat, purring—on steroids.

The mental status of these two big cats from the same environment is remarkable, examples to dispel the myth that all tigers have the same personality. Nikita was bred strictly for entertainment purposes. Sam Mazzola, owner of World Animal Studios, also known as Wildlife Adventures of Ohio, bred Nikita to be used for photo opportunities, dragging the young cub around the Midwest to make large amounts of money.

As soon as cubs such as these open their eyes, they are shuffled to fairs, malls, festivals, carnivals, birthday parties, and TV shows. It's a lucrative business, and each cub has a short window of use, because tigers grow fast and a large cub can seriously hurt a customer. I quickly saw the line for the white tiger cub was triple the size of the line for the orange tiger cub. The white tiger is cursed to be bred over and over to supply the endless demand for "White Magic." Nikita and Nora were victims of this curse.

Nikita was trained, as all Sam's animals were, by being struck with an aluminum ball bat. If anyone went to Sam's facility, you could see a ball bat in almost every corner where the big cats lived. This situation was noted by an animal control officer investigating the facility. He didn't know why they were there until he attended a training session I taught near Cleveland, Ohio. He approached me after the lecture and said, "That explains everything."

In this abusive environment, Nikita festered, survived, and began hating humans, especially men. It was here that Nikita became possibly the most dangerous white tiger in the United States. Tammy Thies, executive director of The Wildcat Sanctuary, was planning to relocate Nikita to her facility, and she needed me to do the prep work to get Nikita ready for her journey to Minnesota. The problem was that I could not get near Nikita.

Our veterinarians had to observe her from a distance, and we all decided not to stress or aggravate her. Denise Flores of Tiger Paws, an exotic rescue center in Ashland, Ohio, was our mediator. Denise and her husband, José, have a unique ability to bond with abused big cats. They originally rescued Nikita and Nora from Sam Mazzola's World Animal Studios, both cats were underweight and malnourished. With their help and good care, we were able to prepare Nikita to be relocated to The Wildcat Sanctuary in Sandstone, Minnesota.

Tammy and her team also came with a plan to relocate Nikita rather than simply put her down as so many other organizations in their place would have. Even I was skeptical. I felt this was going to be a dangerous relocation and was seriously thinking of at least tranquilizing Nikita.

But after watching the patient and calming approach of the relocation team, I was amazed. Nikita was at first her typical snarling and aggressive self, but after a short time she calmed down, and the team was able to get Nikita to enter a transfer cage without incident. We were all stunned and happily surprised. A few years after Nikita left Ohio for

The Wildcat Sanctuary, I was able to pay her a visit.

I did not recognize her. Her disposition was the exact opposite of the white tiger that attacked a man in Cleveland, a transformation caused by the patient and loving care of those at The Wildcat Sanctuary.

―――

Nora was another story. She was also bred for entertainment opportunities at World Animal Studios, and like Nikita, had been rescued by Tiger Paws. Nora was so malnourished the Tiger Paws people feared for her life. Unfortunately, Tiger Paws was having financial problems and could not give Nora the long-term care she needed. That would be done by WildCat Ridge Sanctuary in Oregon.

That was when I received a call from Cheryl Tuller, WildCat Ridge's executive director, who was looking to transport Nora to Oregon. Most big cats needed some type of medical care done before moving, and as Tiger Paws was only three hours away from me, I went because I wanted to help in any way I could.

I didn't really know the couple, only that they had done a good job with Nikita. Denise Flores had originally been nervous about me even being on Tiger Paws' property, but I was used to such suspicions. Many organizations had made outrageous statements about me, which tended to prejudice people against working with me in the first place, especially private owners. Denise and José were members of one of the largest organizations in the Midwest, the Ohio Association of Animal Owners. I am against the private ownership of dangerous wild/exotic animals by untrained people, and OAAO is for it. It was that simple.

With this in mind, I completely understood Denise's reservations. But we were both trying to help Nora who, I quickly learned, had a deer rib bone stuck in her molars. It was stabbing into her cheek, causing severe pain and making it impossible for her to eat. Her moaning was heartbreaking. Her jaw was swollen and the bone was beginning to pierce through it. Denise and I squatted down next to the cage, and Denise kept warning me that Nora could reach through the cage and grab me. Nora, she said, still had her claws.

I tried to calm both Denise and Nora, even though I knew I was going to have to get close to Nora's mouth to get a clear video so that my medical team could determine exactly how to help her. Nora was agitated and rubbing her injured cheek against the cage, moaning and growling in pain. I lay down in the grass next to the cage to try and let Nora get used to me. She pawed at me, not in a vicious way, but as if she was just pleading for help.

Then I reached in and tried to dislodge the rib bone. It loosened but didn't come out. I asked my partner for the video camera. Nora sniffed it and touched it with her paw. She seemed to accept it and me.

I reached gently into the cage and pulled Nora's whiskers up. At first, she pulled back and sneezed. With Denise's help, I did it again and Nora opened her mouth wide. For the first few seconds I had a clear shot at the deer rib wedged between her molars. And I got the video! I did this all while lying on the grass, up against the cage, with Nora looking down at me.

It was the perfect angle to get the footage we needed. I immediately got up and headed to my vehicle. As we were getting into it, Denise wanted to know when we would be coming back. I told her that we would have a medical team in Ashland by the weekend. "Are you really coming back to help?" she asked. "Absolutely," I told her. She grabbed my arm and gave the best compliment I have ever had: "You're not the asshole everyone told me you were." I smiled and replied, "You haven't gotten to know me yet."

Nora, like Nikita, had been cursed at birth because of her color. They made thousands of dollars for Sam Mazzola. Even when they were over two hundred pounds, Sam would sedate them and chain them to a heavy support by a short chain. He did this so his cats could not raise their heads, and the paying customer could sit next to them and be photographed. Nora and Nikita traveled in small cages from town to town, fair to fair, mall to mall. What a miserable life. And when they got too big to handle, they had outlived their usefulness.

The stories of Nora and Nikita were typical of the exploitation and abuse of these cats. People are always asking me how white tigers that originally came to the U.S. as rare, endangered big cats only seen in accredited zoos can end up in a non-accredited, abusive, roadside menagerie near Cleveland, Ohio, owned by the notorious Sam Mazzola. The answer was a remedial one: exploitation and money. It was ironic to me that the lineage of white tigers came directly from Ohio by way of the Cincinnati Zoo, and now we had come full circle, back to a backyard in Ohio.

Nora's predicament ended in a surprising, downright anti-climactic manner. Our medical team decided we should give physicals to the other Oregon-bound tigers while we worked on Nora. Denise called me the day before we were to return and said she was able to pull the rib out of Nora's swollen mouth—with her fingers! (My disclaimer: please do not try this at home.) Nora is a special white tiger, an amazing big cat that has never shown aggression and now lives happily at WildCat Ridge Sanctuary in Oregon.

Cheryl and Mike Tuller made the drive from Oregon to Ohio, then back again, strictly out of the love of these big cats. An amazing trip; an amazing couple.

As for Denise and José, ironically, when they first met me, they thought I had intended to make them an example of untenable wildlife practices. Without realizing it, they proved that they were actually an example of my mission. A good example at that. As a completely unexpected by-product of this incident, I had gained new friends, new allies, and new resources, whose collective goal was to actually live up to the slogans made famous in TV commercials—to actually *save the tigers*.

10

Tiger in a Box

"He was killed for being himself." —Tammy Thies

Tammy Thies and her team have years of experience working with all kinds of big cats, but none of their other experiences were quite like the one with Como, the highly-publicized white tiger who had attacked a seven-year-old girl at a private animal park in Racine, Minnesota, in 2001. The event prompted national headlines and spurred an investigation into the rural zoo that was housing Como—B.E.A.R.C.A.T Hollow.

It was what Tammy called her "first experience into the true captive wildlife crisis and the illegal trade in animal parts," and it was one of the saddest stories she had ever heard. Como's home was called a sanctuary, but it was anything but. It was run by Ken and Nancy Kraft, who bred, sold, bought, and leased animals. Tammy said they even ran a second operation that sold dead tigers.

Then one day, Como somehow got out of its enclosure and attacked the little girl, dragging her several feet. The girl, Emily Hartman, was not seriously injured and Tammy's organization, Wildcat Sanctuary, offered to provide a secure home for Como. The state, however, ruled that the young victim must have rabies shots or Como would be put to death and tested. And in this manner, Como died.

Some good did come from it all. The Krafts were ultimately charged under a federal law outlawing trade in protected animals, and the timing was exquisite: a few days after those charges, they were facing *other* charges; it seems they had sold a tiger to a New Yorker named Antoine Yates, who kept the four-hundred-pound animal in his fifth-floor flat in Harlem—and had been mauled by it. (When officials went to the apartment to retrieve the tiger, they also found a five-foot alligator. Mr. Yates was believed to be the first animal-lover to think of operating a high-rise zoo.)

A federal grand jury in Minneapolis indicted the Krafts for tampering with witnesses, falsifying paperwork, and conspiring to sell and buy more than $200,000 in endangered or threatened animals in interstate commerce. All of it was prompted by Como's attack on the little girl. The Krafts pled guilty; Ken Kraft received an eighteen-month sentence, his wife fifteen months.

―――

While greatly saddened by what had happened to Como, there would be a coda for Tammy—and it would bring back all those earlier events. Because in 2016, she walked into her office and found a large cardboard box waiting for her. "Interstate Meat Dist., Inc." was written on its side. "It stopped me in my tracks," she would write. "As I approached, a wave of emotion came over me. One so strong, it made my heart heavy, made it hard to breathe and my pulse began to race."

She didn't understand her own emotion, nor why she was feeling so unsettled. It was nothing new for Wildcat

Sanctuary to receive such things as donated pelts and/or mounted animals from people who didn't know what else to do with them. But this one didn't feel like those. It felt personal and painful.

She asked the office manager to help her open the box and explained to her, "I don't know why, but I feel connected to whatever is in this box." Inside was a white tiger pelt, and she began weeping. She knew instantly what—who—it was. It was Como, and Tammy was immediately thrust a decade and a half into her past. A law firm had found the pelt in a storage room and, thinking that it might be of some educational use—and knowing nothing of her connection to Como—sent the pelt off to The Wildcat Sanctuary.

"So," she wrote, "how could I prove this shell of a tiger in front of me was Como? And why was I so determined to know? It's because no tiger should be bred to be kept in a roadside zoo or sold as a pet..." Como, she said, had been sentenced to a life in captivity, and he was killed simply for being himself.

"Seeing Como again this way was heart wrenching," she said. "They had preserved the skin on the head, whiskers, even the pads on his feet and back claws. His front feet had been declawed, but the pelt even had the sad regrowth we see in poorly declawed captive cats. And then there it was. Boldly in front of me, written in a marker was one word. It said, *Krafts*.

All her instincts had been confirmed. It *was* Como. He had been killed, skinned, and put in a box. He deserved respect, she said, and she wrote down his story. "He's here for me to tell you his story," she said, "and the story of all of the other animals that suffered in the system..."

"Once I tell this story, I can finally put Como to rest. He, along with all the other donated pelts, receive the same respect and freedom as our residents. He will be cremated and his ashes will be spread across wildlife land where he will spend the rest of forever—free as he was meant to be."

11

How Much is that Tiger in the Window?

Purchasing a tiger, white or orange, is even less difficult than renting one.

In the not-too-distant past, big cats and other exotic animals have, quite literally, been sold right out of store windows. An American phenomenon is the rental of white tigers, as well as their orange brothers and sisters, for special family events. Tigers are featured at every event from weddings to birthday parties, from Bar Mitzvahs to family reunions, and even for high school graduation photos. My favorite misuse involves a provider/animal pimp renting a tiger to a couple preparing for their wedding.

All anyone has to do is get on the internet, google "rent or buy a tiger," and choose a site. It is quite probably more difficult to rent a car than a white tiger. At least the car rental service demands you have a license to drive and a valid ID. All a bride and groom would need is cash or a credit card, and they can rent the largest predatory big cat in the world, the ultimate killing machine, ready to mingle with your wedding guests and family. No experience needed.

When I was in Nepal helping with a tiger project in the wild, I told some of the Nepalese tiger researchers that, in the U.S., untrained people can rent or buy a tiger. They swore I was lying, or at least exaggerating. When I showed them the proof, they were both disgusted and shocked.

Naïve renters have the tiger brought into their neighborhoods. Their neighbors might never know this perfect killing machine was living or visiting next door. From personal experience, I know that the local public safety department will usually not know until there is an escape, or a person attacked and injured. It is illegal to bring dynamite to a wedding. Why is it legal to bring a thinking, mobile IED (improvised explosive device), complete with fangs and claws, into a wedding?

One such wedding was the one of rapper and TV celebrity, 2 Chainz and Kesha Ward. Kanye West, Lil Wayne, Kim Kardashian, and other celebrities were part of the wedding party at the famed Versace Mansion in Miami, Florida. The couple spent over $300,000 on the wedding with the festive highlight being a young adult white tiger.

The stressed tiger was brought out in a portable cage for all the guests to get a photo with and gawk at. This wedding is not unusual, nor is it the first to exploit a tiger. Unfortunately, in the American culture it seems mandatory for popular musicians, professional athletes, and movie stars/TV entertainers to have themselves photographed with a tiger.

Ironically, the celebrities who promote and do commercials and film educational programs on the conservation of these animals also have had selfies with tigers at questionable facilities. And some of them use live tigers in their movies or TV programs. Kaley Cuoco has done a commercial for a major animal conservation group instructing viewers to stop exploiting animals. There are also selfies of her with big cat cubs.

Photos of Kaley Cuoco were taken at her thirtieth birthday celebration held at the notorious Black Jaguar-White Tiger private menagerie owned by Eduardo Serio. Eduardo calls his home and compound a wildlife sanctuary, but a true sanctuary does not breed (even by accident, as he professed), or do photo opportunities for money with a constant stream of big cat cubs seen on his Facebook/website, which is filled with big cat selfies and interactions with celebrities and visitors.

Eduardo has said that he does not breed, and I say, "Someone sure does." He also has said that what he does is not illegal, and I say, "It may be legal, but it sure as heck is not right."

Celebrity selfies with big cats are not just popular but can be used by the exploiters to pull in lots of donation money. Who doesn't want a photo with a big cat cub? Mike Tyson has done it, even buying tigers as pets. Justin Bieber has been photographed with an adult white tiger on a leash. Tyga, a famous rapper whose name plays off of the word tiger—what a homophone—has done it. Cleveland Browns top draft choice, Baker Mayfield, posed with an adult tiger next to a Rolls Royce (which was also white).

Purchasing a tiger, white or orange, is even less difficult than renting one. Tiger cubs are sold on the internet and exotic animal auctions are held throughout the U.S. Interested buyers do not have to be a biologist or a zoologist;

they can live in an apartment, a home in the city, or in a suburban neighborhood. And these cubs end up in corn cribs, basements, garages, makeshift kennels, and poorly constructed cages. Many purchased tigers escape when they get too big to manage safely. This happens because the caring but misinformed owners have no idea how to build a safe, escape-proof habitat.

Many accredited facilities and zoos have had tigers escape, oftentimes to kill or injure someone, and *they* are the professionals. How in the world is it okay to let an untrained person buy a dangerous animal? Why is there no national regulation to protect the big cats, owners, the public, and the first responders?

Your house cat has to have vaccinations to live safely in your neighborhood. The largest predatory big cat in the world does not have the same regulations as Fluffy the house cat. If house cat owners are bitten by their own cat and have to go to the emergency room, paperwork must be filled out for the local health district. Fluffy has to be quarantined. It is even worse if Fluffy scratches or bites a friend or neighbor.

If your pet tiger does the same thing, there are no laws or regulations requiring anyone to do anything. There should at least be regulations to protect the public from the potential zoonotic diseases, although the tiger is likely in more danger from its human contacts.

12

Cash for Cats

"Eco or ego." —David Enden

David Enden, who grew up in a small town on Long Island's north shore and spent his childhood rescuing injured wildlife, is the leader of a new breed of animal advocates. David comes armed with a professional science master's degree in zoo, aquarium and animal shelter management from Colorado State University, diverse experience in everything from eco-tourism to big cats, and great passion. He's known for his eloquent TED talk on tigers, as well as an essay, "The Socioeconomics of the White Tiger," which gives an unusually astute picture of the isolated world of the white tiger in America.

He not only uses his heart but his head, too. Knowing that David is working to protect these animals, following the mission to teach proper behavior around wildlife, makes it comforting for me to pass the torch to him. I can leave knowing that he will continue the good fight. The big cats are in good hands.

David's timeline for the white tiger begins in 1960 when the first white tiger in America arrived at the National Zoo in Washington, DC. This, of course, was Mohini, who came from the first litter of white tigers born in captivity, courtesy the Maharaja of Rewa who, according to the Bandhavgahr National Park, captured Mohini's father, Mohan, and raised him in the Maharaja's court.

When Mohan's daughter appeared in America, she was regarded, as David points out, "our planet's unicorn species." But Mohini was the product of old Mohan and Mohan's daughter, Radha, who carried her father's white gene. And here was the irony, for not only was Mohini a product of inbreeding, but so were her offspring. At the time, little was known of the white tigers' biology, nor of the genetic infirmities that would come from inbreeding.

The white tiger, of course, was a natural occurrence in the wild, which is how it was first discovered. It is mal-adaptive in forested areas, but can be beneficial in a winter wonderland, David explains. The issue is the presence of deformities, which do *not* come from the genes for the white coat, but in the inbreeding process, which has been scientifically traced and tested. "In breeding, sometimes certain traits are connected to the same genetic code. For example, in Russia when scientists attempted to breed for a tame fox, they wound up with an animal that looked like a dog. It turns out that tameness was genetically linked to many of the physical traits of our domestic dogs. We see this all the time. In the case of the white tiger, the genetic code is rare. So in order to produce it, we can increase the probability of white tiger offspring by inbreeding. The inbreeding, like in any animal, is what causes the genetic deformities."

David sees the inbreeding as quickly producing a line of tigers that were fascinating in their unusual appearance, but their genetic flaws were not as easily seen and, in so many cases, disregarded. He thinks that the fundamental moment occurred when the Cincinnati Zoo borrowed Mohini's daughter, Kesari, and bred cubs that were bought by Siegfried and Roy for their Las Vegas act.

"The novel sight of these three majestic pure white tigers, combined with the performance of magic, was a bone-chilling experience of awe that would forever transform the concept of animals in entertainment," he wrote. "Any industry database will state that 'new attractions' are the leading source of revenue for the amusement park and entertainment industry. As bootstrapping entrepreneurs, Siegfried and Roy spent the majority of their career traveling worldwide and scraping to make ends meet. It wasn't until their purchase of the white tiger in 1983 that they were on their way to being known in 1988 as 'the greatest show in the history of Las Vegas.'"

The heightened visibility of the animals quickly spread across a range of economic venues: roadside zoos, circuses, truck stops, then into commercial trade shows, VIP gatherings, and product launches. Vegas, ironically, had supplied the demand. In not much more than a few decades, old Mohan's turf had gone from the jungles of India to his descendants, whose turf was set artificially in the jungles of commerce.

Once the demand was set, more tigers were bred, in what David calls "a puppy mill-like scenario." The market had expanded into "a more residential form of private ownership" that David thinks caused the leap in tiger ownership in the final decade of the last century. It was fueled by the personal aggrandizement of entertainment figures, particularly macho figures in boxing and football, many of them with millions of followers on social media platforms wherein the tiger is used as a prop.

Oddly, social media falls on both sides of tiger conservation: it provides an unlimited platform for education; however while its glamorous selfies and other photos present fanciful images that magnify the exploitation. "Social media," David says, "has been a nightmare for those of us fighting to end the exploitation of iconic wildlife and endangered species…celebrity influencers, videos and pictures of novel experiences, and the lack of welfare knowledge in the public has exponentially increased poor decision making."

Meanwhile, the tiger had become nothing more than "a product listed on Craigslist. Unchecked by laws and regulations, breeding facilities and private owners created a lucrative market for buying and selling the genetic cocktail of an endangered species we now call the American Tiger."

David thinks the driving force behind the supply-and-demand economics for white tigers is a basic sociological concept: the need to belong. For the wealthy, he says, it's a competition of glamour and status, elevating celebrities even among themselves. When Kim Kardashian visited Black Jaguar-White Tiger, regarded by many conservationists as a "pseudo-sanctuary," attendance shot up. A product of the Paris Hilton Rule—"famous for being famous"—Kardashian has more than a hundred million followers on Instagram, and, says David, "her massive following will not only view full contact tiger interactions as something okay to do, but as an important goal in achieving similar social status."

While some see this as an attempt at peer-ingathering and belonging, others see it as heightened aggrandizement, a kind of competitive one-upmanship endowed so recklessly by social media. And both bolster David's point about the difficulty of using social media educationally.

The larger conservation problem is the overarching problem of ecosystems, particularly in developing countries where, as David writes, "the root issues of deforestation and human-wildlife conflict have not been solved." Conservationists have long argued for the preservation of tiger populations because as apex predators—they have no natural predators, that is, except us—they're bellwethers for the ecosystem in which they live. They actually keep such systems stable, controlling other populations under them and thereby preserving a balance between herbivores and the vegetation they eat. Says the website Sciencing, "Where tigers succeed, food webs remain intact and ecosystems remain stable."

In the final analysis, though, as Anthony Barnosky, the director of Stanford University's Jasper Ridge Biological Preserve, says, the reason for saving the tigers may have less to do with either ecosystem or the tourist economy, "but simply because they are magnificent creatures. We have a moral and ethical imperative to save them in the wild. "I don't want to be part of a generation that destroyed the last wild tiger."

13

Canned Cats

A mystical object of power and machismo.

The lure of "White Magic" entices people from all cultures and walks of life. Yes, there are the people who make large amounts of money exploiting tigers, but there are also people who have other reasons. There are, for instance, those who see the white tiger as a mystical object of power and machismo. To them, being photographed with the world's most powerful big cat seems to symbolize that *they* have the same qualities as the tiger.

This symbolism has gone on for centuries, from primitive times until now. It is deep in the human psyche, from historically wearing tiger hides, claws, and teeth to show strength, to modern times when one has a photo taken with a tiger. The selfie shows one's friends how "brave" they are, getting so close to a large predator.

Many of us have evolved to the understanding that this practice is abusive. We now have to gently push our fellow humans toward this same understanding. We have to be careful not to constantly condemn an unknowing public, rather show them the truth and let them decide to change. This is how real progress happens.

Breeders and pay-to-play exploiters should be exposed and condemned for their abusive practices. They know what they are doing is wrong. If they truly loved these tigers—as they claim to the public that they do—they would be the first ones to stop this cruel practice.

Others think they are *saving* the endangered tiger. They are saving them by buying them and raising them in their homes, which follows the hype spouted by the animal 'conservationists' on the TV talk shows about how keeping them in captivity is saving the wild tigers. These good-hearted people think if they can do their small part by raising tigers in their homes, they can help save the tiger. I know. I was one of them.

For the last forty-five years, I've asked tiger owners, "Why did you get your tiger?" They would say, "To help save the tiger!" These are the good people who, when they realize that the hype was a lie, now have a four-hundred-pound tiger living in a twenty-by-twenty corn crib in their backyard, and eventually they reach out to me to help them find a place for their beloved tiger.

These rescues and relocations are always emotionally traumatic to the owners, as well as the rescuers. The owner realizes that they made a huge mistake and feels immense guilt. Rescuers should always be understanding, caring for the owner as well as the tiger. This behavior helps create an ally. For the owner will now be able to speak to and comfort fellow owners who want to relocate their tigers. They can also tell others about their dilemma and perhaps talk any future owners out of buying a tiger cub.

There are the tiger owners who have gone to the exotic animal auctions to specifically buy their new pet because they've always wanted one. These owners perhaps have a dream of becoming like their TV 'conservationist' heroes. Some of them call themselves "Tiger Man" or "King of Tigers." They wear shirts and coats with their new moniker on them, so everyone who sees them will know who they are and ask questions. They become local celebrities.

Even this small celebrity status is like a drug. Just a little bit of fame can be addicting—and also dangerous. These are the owners who usually get mauled by showing off. Even worse, they may get innocent visitors hurt. These are the most dangerous owners. The old adage that a little bit of knowledge is dangerous seriously pertains to them. Then there are the black market tiger breeders and suppliers. They are even worse than the pay-to-play exploiters.

These are the people who breed, buy, and supply the black market for tiger parts. The mysterious black market is not only the well-publicized Chinese medicinal market, but the U.S. and European market for hides and taxidermy specimens for personal collections.

Even sadder are the canned hunts in which unwanted ex-pets become prey themselves, with hunters paying thousands of dollars to shoot a hand-raised tiger in an enclosure. These tigers are easy to kill because they have been hand fed and raised by humans their entire lives. When a jeep drives into the small, fenced-in area, the tigers immediately respond in a positive manner, sometimes walking right up to the vehicle.

The tigers do not realize that the humans who have cared for them are now allowing someone to kill them. I say it is like hunting in a petting zoo. You go up to a machine for a handful of food, coax a deer to come up to eat, then—BOOM!—you shoot them. The height of sportsmanship, yes? I know of no real hunter or outdoor sportsmen who would support these canned hunt executions. Yet these killing fields exist in South Africa and they are even scattered across the U.S.

The Chinese tiger parts market is the most infamous. Tigers are killed and everything is used from their penises, claws, skin, and teeth to their ground up bones. Every part of a tiger is used for some medicinal "purpose." The tiger parts supposedly do everything from curing a gallbladder problem to giving a man a better erection. This is all a myth, but in China and Chinatowns around the world, it is gospel. Grinding up tiger bones does not cure any ailment in humans, but many pet tigers end up as "medicine," with wild tigers the most sought after, and prices tripling for a dead one. It is a billion-dollar business, and another example of selfish desires built upon the extermination of a species.

In the U.S., ranchers and park rangers exterminated the grey wolf from Yellowstone National Park only a few generations ago. They were slaughtered because they were allegedly competing with their hunting and ranching.

We have evolved to know that was not the truth. Man's ignorant myths caused the demise of the wolf. The same is happening to the tiger, especially the white ones.

Educating new generations has been effective for the wolves but does not seem to have slowed the tiger black market. A tiger is still worth more dead than alive. It amazes me that allegedly educated and enlightened celebrities, sports heroes, conservationists, and private owners cannot figure out that these big cats have been sentenced to a life of exploitation and confinement without having done any crime.

Russ Clear, my partner and long-time friend, said it best during the filming of *The Elephant in the Living Room*. Russ was my right-hand man when I was working with people and their dangerous animal pets. He did everything from welding cages to entertaining people along the way with his muscles and personality. Russ was a member of the Christian-based Faith Force, entertaining kids and civic groups with feats of strength, such as breaking ball bats with his hands and smashing cement blocks with his head. Standing six-foot-three and weighing 310 pounds, Russ was a six-time world bench press and strict curl champion, one of the most powerful and intimidating men in the world but also the most compassionate and loving to all God's creatures.

Russ, a former enforcer for the Hells Angels who'd spent time in San Quentin for murder, did not know I overheard him talking through the cage to the male lion, Lambert. Through eyes filled with tears he whispered to Lambert, "I know why I had to be put in a cage; I understand what you are going through. You have done nothing wrong. People have caged you and stolen your God-given right to be free and wild."

The celebrities could learn a thing or two from the words Russ whispered quietly in a private conversation with a caged lion, which was a message to all of us.

14

The Good, the Bad, and the Ugly

"I'm the Joker then!" —Joe Exotic

Speaking out against the exploitation of tigers has actually proven to be a dangerous endeavor for me, as well as for those with whom I work. I have had a number of threats through the years. They have ranged from the veiled and obscure, such as a hangman's noose hanging from my vehicle, to blatant, outright threats to kill me and my family.

One of the biggest offenders in the cub breeding/exploitation/death threat game is Joe Exotic. Joe's true name is Joseph Schreibvogel but he is also known as Joseph Maldonado-Passage, Aarron Alex, Cody Ryan, and others. It seemed that whenever Joe got in legal trouble, he changed his name, hence the multiplicity of aliases.

He was the owner of the Greater Wynnewood Exotic Animal Park in Wynnewood, Oklahoma, which has been called "one of the most notorious cub petting roadside zoos in the country."

He also had a traveling exhibit, taking cubs to malls across the middle of the country. The *Daily Mail* reported that Joe charged $16 for customers to play with his tigers and that he'd posted a video on his business website in which he shot the tigers with tranquilizer darts. The Wynnewood zoo itself has been criticized by animal rights groups from the Humane Society of the United States to People for the Ethical Treatment of Animals, in addition to being investigated more than once by the Department of Agriculture.

Joe had a nonstop public relations campaign advertising himself. This included various runs for political office, including an ill-fated run for president in 2016 when he was an independent candidate using YouTube to post videos. (John Oliver, host of HBO's late-night talk and news satire program, profiled Joe and other "alternative" candidates in 2016, where he said, "Joe Exotic is truly the candidate you'd want to sit down and have a beer with, then another beer, and then several more beers until you're drunk enough to try meth for the first time.")

Joe repeatedly showed on his TV program various images of him shooting effigies of big cat advocates with nonstop threats of "I am going to take you out," or "I am going to put a cap in his ass," or "I am going to permanently shut you up." On one occasion, Joe and I were being interviewed by a national TV network over our battle against each other on regulations and laws about ownership of big cats by untrained people. Joe thinks anyone should be able to buy and own a big cat. I do not. During the interview, the correspondent asked me why we needed regulations. As I was responding, the interviewer made a remark that I was like Batman swooping in to protect these animals. She was referencing the most popular movie at that time, *The Dark Knight.*

Before I could respond, Joe Exotic swooped in, put his face in front of the camera, and screamed, "Then I am the Joker!" He mugged for the viewing audience, sticking out his tongue and laughing maniacally. We were all stunned, but this was the true Joe Exotic.

In September of 2018, to put all of this in context, a federal grand jury returned an indictment accusing Joe "Exotic" Maldonado-Passage of hiring an unnamed person to murder a "Jane Doe" in Florida. Joe was subsequently arrested by the FBI, U.S. Marshals, and local authorities in the town of Gulf Breeze, Florida.

His arrest was not a surprise to me, nor to most of my colleagues. The arrest did surprise the general public, who had no idea that this big cat breeding and exploitation was going on. A colleague and fellow big cat advocate, Carole Baskin, CEO of the internationally known Big Cat Rescue, has been the most vocal advocate in fighting the private, unregulated breeding and exploitation of big cats in the country. Her focus was on large, private breeding facilities, and to her, GW Exotic Animal Park was the largest offender in the U.S.

Joe Exotic was the flamboyant, abrasive owner, and when Carole began exposing Joe for what he truly was—an "animal pimp"—he began his verbal assault on Carole and Big Cat Rescue. At one point, in a video posted online, Joe says to the camera, "Carole Baskin better never, ever, ever see me face-to-face. Ever, ever, ever again." Then he picked up a gun and fired it in to the head of a blonde-haired doll obviously meant to be Carole.

The battle went on for years, with Carole and Howard (her husband) fighting back with facts, countering the many lies, personal attacks, and verbal redirections from

Joe. Carole had warned Joe to cease and desist his defamation of character attacks. Joe thumbed his nose and continued. His violent threats and character assassination of other groups usually backed them off. But Carole and Howard Baskin did *not* back off.

Big Cat Rescue notified malls across the Midwest and Southwest, describing the conditions under which Joe's animals tried to exist, which affected Joe's business. Joe retaliated by renaming his organization after Carole's—"Big Cat Rescue Entertainment." Then Carole and Howard sued for violation of intellectual property rights. In 2013, they were awarded a $1 million settlement. Joe persisted by making a video in which he said, "For Carole and all of her friends that are watching out there, if you think for one minute I was nuts before, I am the most dangerous exotic animal owner on this planet right now. And before you bring me down, it is my belief that you will stop breathing."

Joe's rants became more personal and violent, and as a retired law enforcement officer, I began to seriously worry for Carole and Howard's safety. Joe, in his own words, had become the poster child for dangerous, narcissistic behavior. The signs and symptoms were obvious. And when a person like Joe is backed into a corner, his next response is usually violence. In the summer of 2018, *The Oklahoman* reported that Joe sold most of his gun collection. Except for his AR-15 assault rifle. That, he is said to have explained, "is for Carole."

Joe's verbal attacks and lies had finally caught up with him, and he had no other way of retribution except to resort to the most drastic of measures: he tried to hire a hit man to kill Carole Baskin, the "Jane Doe" in his indictment. But somehow in Joe's tangled processes, he ended up making his requests for the hit to an undercover FBI agent.

The upshot? Exotic Joe was indicted for the alleged and equally exotic murder-for-hire of one Jane Doe. "Jane Doe" was, of course, Carole Baskin. In a video message she said, "It is important to understand that this is not the isolated act of one crazy bad apple...Big Cat Rescue has been a leader in working to stop what we view as abuse of big cats and we have been very effective in our work. I have received multiple death threats over the years, including at one point a number of snakes placed in my mailbox."

The irony of Joe's downward slide was not lost on me and the genuine animal rescue organizations: Joe, through his inexplicable actions, had made *himself* into something of an endangered species.

15

Character Assassination

This myth haunts me to this day.

The charges against Joe Exotic were no surprise because I, too, had experienced his character assassinations. For years, he had spread outrageous lies about me. Joe and the other exotic animal breeders/exploiters lashed out at me when a fellow firefighter, Michael Peterman, died from a venomous snake bite in Dayton, Ohio.

I worked in the neighboring city of Oakwood where we had mutual aid medic runs into Dayton. On major fire calls, Dayton Fire had similar runs into Oakwood. Michael and I had worked together on some of these runs, and I knew of his love of snakes. Michael was on the scene when a sixteen-foot Burmese python was loose in downtown Dayton, and I responded to help. It was somebody's pet and it had gotten out. It was found in a parking lot beside a restaurant. Michael and I put it in a large plastic trashcan and found it a home in a zoo. ("I wondered why no one was coming in to eat," said the restaurant manager.)

I knew Michael had a collection of snakes at his home. But what I did not know was that he had venomous snakes in his personal collection. These snakes, including rattlesnakes and even a Rhino viper from Africa, were in an upstairs bedroom in a heavily populated Dayton neighborhood.

It worries me when people have dangerous exotic animals in their homes. What happens if there is a fire? The responding firefighters wouldn't know of the deadly situation as they are going about their work.

Michael was bitten by a Rhino viper and taken to the local trauma center by his own crew members. Generally speaking, hospitals do not have antivenom on hand for exotic venomous snake bites. I always had the most updated protocol for venomous snake bites with me at all times because of my own particular experience with such reptiles. I had captured and relocated every type of snake from cobras to Gaboon vipers, and I needed to have the protocol with me as a precautionary measure.

―

While I was focused on saving my friend and co-worker, I missed out on a valuable personal lesson until it was too late. Sadly, if you—as the person with first-hand knowledge of a tragic situation like this—won't talk to the media, they will find someone who will, regardless of that source's factual, or lack of factual, knowledge of the same incident.

We had contacted a venom extraction facility in Kentucky, which immediately sent vials of polyvalent antivenom for African vipers to the Dayton Trauma Center by Aircare helicopter out of Cincinnati. The ER doctors administered the antivenom to Michael, who had not been breathing for an extended period of time. The medical term is hypoxia. In other words, there was not enough oxygen in the tissues to sustain the patient's bodily functions.

Yet he responded to the dose administered, was stabilized, and flown to a Cincinnati hospital where a well-known venom specialist was a responding doctor. (Aircare will not transport a patient unless they are stable and potentially viable.) Since I had done all I could for him there, I immediately went back to Michael's house, captured the Rhino viper, and put it into a secure transport cage.

The media, meanwhile, was hounding us for the story. But I had made the decision not to speak, out of respect for Michael and his family. Since neither ER doctors nor I spoke to the media, the media went to other sources. These sources were not involved and had no knowledge of what happened. A rescue team from Florida that had antivenom immediately jumped at the chance to get its fifteen minutes of fame.

The Florida team blasted all media outlets that they were heroically flying antivenom from Miami, Florida, to Dayton, Ohio, to "save a fellow firefighter's life." The ER doctors told them Michael had already been given the antivenom and there was no need for them to fly to Dayton. That did not stop them. The next day, Michael was found to have no brain activity. The Florida rescuers told anyone that wanted to hear that Michael Peterman died because he did not get the "lifesaving antivenom" they wanted to fly up.

They basically led the public to believe that ignorant medical professionals in Ohio caused Michael's death. By the time I recognized that the world thought Michael died from our neglect, it was too late for me to counter the lie.

Michael's family and co-workers knew exactly what we did to try to save him. I received a letter of commendation from the Dayton Fire Department for my part in trying to save Michael and for capturing the deadly snake. The truth, however, did not mean anything.

I learned to immediately speak to the media after a dangerous incident. Now because of the misinformation blindly printed in newspapers and magazines and reported on TV shows, the public believed we allowed Michael to die.

―

The media's baseless story of what happened to Michael Peterman was wonderful ammunition for exploiters like Joe Exotic, just as I was trying to get regulations on private ownership of dangerous wild/exotic animals in my state of Ohio. Joe and his followers labeled me a murderer, echoing to officials that I let Michael die so that I could have another Ohio-death-by-exotic-animal statistic.

There were three other human deaths by dangerous pets in Ohio the year of Michael's death, yet there were some government officials who would not talk to me because they believed the misinformation propaganda. And why wouldn't they? Media outlets from *The New York Times* to the *Los Angeles Times* had printed that I was part of the reason why Michael died.

This baseless accusation follows me to this day. I have had senators and state representatives ask me if I was the guy who had killed Michael Peterman. It was my first taste of the vicious lying and brutal fabrications of Joe Exotic and the rest of the 'conservationists'. But it was certainly not the last.

Michael Peterman died in 2003. In 2011, I went through another round of fabrications and lies, again over the death of an exotic animal owner. It happened this time after the Zanesville Massacre in Zanesville, Ohio.

Terry Thompson had a farm outside Zanesville, near Interstate 70, and a collection of the most dangerous exotic animals in the world: thirty-eight big cats (tigers, African lions, mountain lions, and leopards), multiple species of bears, primates, and wolves. He was also selling firearms illegally. Terry was arrested by Federal agents and local law enforcement, convicted, and sentenced to prison.

In Ohio at this time, there were no laws to prevent the private ownership of dangerous exotic animals. Ironically, Terry could have the world's largest predatory big cat, but it was illegal for him to own or sell certain firearms. Before Terry was sentenced in court, he told everyone that when he got out of prison he would turn all his animals loose and kill himself.

When Terry was finally released, he did exactly what he had promised to do: he turned fifty-six of the most dangerous exotic animals loose, cut all the fencing of the cages so the responding public safety teams could not put them back, then shot himself in the head. This was how the first responding officer found him, except two white tigers were eating him.

Sadly, forty-nine of the animals had to be shot by law enforcement and killed to protect public safety. It was rainy, near-dark, and dart rifles would not have worked. It is dangerous to dart a large predator in the dark, because now they would have a drug-crazed tiger running through your neighborhood. It can take up to fifteen minutes to successfully sedate a big cat or bear, and that is only if you correctly guessed the weight of the animal. One of the drugs used is ketamine. Called "Special K" by partiers on the streets and in rave clubs, it can magnify all your senses and cause a neurological reaction. This is *not* what you want to do to a four-hundred-pound adrenaline-overdosed big cat.

When morning came, the aftermath was horrific. Dead animal bodies were everywhere. Even more stunning was to see these big cats and other exotic predators lying dead on a farm in Ohio—not Africa or Asia. This scene to me was surreal and perverted.

⌒

While this nightmare was unfolding, Joe Exotic and his supporters immediately hit the media with a wild story of conspiracy and murder. Joe, of course, did not reach out to help or comfort the remaining animals, or even the emotionally-injured first responders. He was busy telling anyone that would listen that there was only one man in Ohio that could have turned those dangerous animals loose, murdered Terry, and then gotten safely off the property. That man was Tim Harrison. Me.

Once again, I was too busy at first to even realize or keep track of the crimes that Joe Exotic and his followers would subsequently accuse me of committing. I was there shortly after the initial shooting to assist. Terry and I had not seen eye-to-eye on his private ownership of so many dangerous exotic animals. According to Joe, however, the disagreement had not stopped there. According to Joe, I had murdered Terry, and this quickly became a new story line for the incident.

Joe even wrote a song, and the first video for his song featured a silhouette of a man, resembling me with a ball cap on, forcing an actor that looked like Terry to get on his knees, then shooting him in the head, assassination style.

The music video has me turning the animals loose and cutting the cage fencing. I immediately contacted an attorney, and he went after Joe and his production company.

Joe pulled the music video with my likeness and made a new one. The new video showed two police officers, in silhouette, assassinating Terry. Joe did not want the truth to interfere with his conspiracy circus. *That* video was also pulled after law enforcement officials lodged a complaint of their own.

Nothing about the truth fit Joe's farcical vision. This was the Joe Exotic I knew and had to deal with over the years. Bold lies and conspiracies are his bread and butter. He was a huge player in the curse of the white tiger. He not only bred white and orange tigers, he also bred mixed tigers/African lions (tigons, ligers, etc.), for private breeders and tiger exploiters. He fought any law or legislation aimed at protecting big cats and other animals, and was the very face of White Magic. He was the face of tiger cub photo-ops around the country. He admittedly bred hundreds of big cats, mostly tigers, and had the largest collection of tigers and tigons/ligers in the world. A literal tiger "puppy" mill.

He calls himself The Tiger King and proudly promoted himself through song and media. If stopped by Carole Baskin and Big Cat Rescue, he stands to lose everything. If he is defeated by regulations and laws, his business as he knows it will be defeated.

Joe's self-promoted, sociopathic behavior causes him to be dangerous, but even more dangerous is his thousands of followers. He's now a martyr in their eyes. I have been watching his supporters make remarks like, "We all wish he (Joe) would have gotten rid of her (Carole)," and "She was just the start." His paranoid rants have caused an unknown amount of craziness. At first, I did not think Joe actually believed what he was saying, but now I have had a wake-up call. Between his attempts at everything from slanderous hit-pieces on me and actually attempting to hire a hit-man, it has been (and continues to be) something of a wild ride.

There is a lot of bad and ugly in the world of white tigers and big cats. Many times we only see the bad and ugly, but there is still much good happening too. For every Joe Exotic, there is a Carole Baskin to stand up to them. Big Cat Rescue is a facility that has not only rescued big cats but is the leader in investigations, regulations/laws, research gathering, and education. And it goes face-to-face with big cat exploiters and abusers.

During my years working with big cats, I have had the pleasure to work with some amazing organizations: Lions, Tigers and Bears, Alpine, California (Bobby Brink); Black Pine Animal Sanctuary, Albion, Indiana (Lori Gagen); WildCat Ridge Sanctuary, Scotts Mills, Oregon (Cheryl and Mike Tuller); The Wildcat Sanctuary, Sandstone, Minnesota (Tammy Thies); Turpentine Creek Wildlife Refuge, Eureka Springs, Arkansas (Tanya and Scott Smith); The Wild Animal Sanctuary, Keenesburg, Colorado (Pat Craig); Big Cat Rescue, Tampa, Florida (Carole and Howard Baskin); Tiger Haven, Kingston, Tennessee (Mary Haven); and all the members of the Big Cat Sanctuary Alliance.

These organizations and people have risked their lives and endured financial hardship to build and maintain facilities for big cats. These are the groups that have been involved in cleaning up the horrific mess people like Joe Exotic and other animal pimps have caused. These are the true big cat heroes who live with the danger of working with the world's most dangerous big cats every day but also putting up with threats from people like Joe. They are the last resort for big cats that have outgrown their usefulness or attacked their private owners—the big cats no one wants or cares about. The surgically altered, deformed, and mentally unstable.

What amazes me the most is the pure love and compassion they show each big cat that has to be rescued or relocated to their facilities. No one is getting rich in this field of endeavor, but the rewards are what they work so hard for. (Rescuers assert that providing food and vet care to a big cat costs about $10,000 a year.) What are the rewards? The reward is to take a scared, aggressive, under-fed tiger and transform her into a relaxed, confident, mentally strong animal.

This happens by way of a technique big cat exploiters and private breeders do not apparently know: tender, loving care. These sanctuaries do not allow breeding, exploitation, or handling of the big cats. Currently these facilities have unified to be able to help more big cats. This unification is the Big Cat Sanctuary Alliance, a powerful team of people who care but also act. They do not complain that a river is dirty; they work to clean it up. And they know the word *advocate* is also a verb.

16

Where are the Laws?

*Laws and regulations are only good
if they are enforceable.*

The most asked question I get is "Why are there no laws to protect white tigers?" Here is where the smoke and mirrors, the sleight of hand, comes into play. There *are* laws and regulations in effect but they are hindered and sometimes nullified by loopholes strategically placed in to them. The Foreign Species and U.S. Endangered Species Act was passed in 1973 to prevent the extinction of foreign animals and plants. With some exceptions, "the act prohibits certain activities with these protected species unless authorized by a permit from the U.S. Fish and Wildlife Service."

These permits are written so vaguely—"other activities that are consistent," or "activities that would enhance the propagation"—making it easy for backyard breeding of tigers under the guidance of accredited animal conservationists for their personal use.

This is how white tigers like Nora and Nikita ended up in an Ohio backyard. There is also a captive-bred wildlife registration: a person or institution in the U.S. may buy and sell endangered or threatened animals in order to enhance the propagation of a listed species. Key words for a good loophole: "in order to enhance the propagation of a listed species."

These listed big cats, however, have never been bred to return to the wild. They have never been bred to "save the tigers" in India. They are bred for exhibition and entertainment. Here is my favorite paragraph from the U. S. Fish and Wildlife Service: "While the Service discourages keeping listed species as pets, permits are *not* (emphasis mine) required to keep or breed endangered or threatened animals as pets provided that you are not attempting to carry out any prohibited activities."

But using protected species as pets is *not* consistent with the purpose of the act. What smoke and mirrors. This act was supposed to protect listed species but cannot. The act has no bite, and now we have thousands of tigers in private hands, scattered across the landscape.

⁓

The Animal Welfare Act (AWA) was signed into law in 1966—the only federal law in the United States that regulates the treatment of animals in research, exhibition, transport, and by dealers. Other laws, policies, and guidelines may include additional species coverage or specifications for animal care and use, but all refer to the Animal Welfare Act as the minimum acceptable standard.

The act is enforced by USDA, APHIS, and Animal Care. AWA requires that "minimum standards of care and treatment be provided," which is the key phrase here. A tiger can live in a "minimum" cage—a corn crib for example—for its entire life. The big cat will then by law have minimum care and treatment. The word "minimum" means "the least or smallest amount or quantity possible, attainable, or required." Visualize a five-hundred-pound big cat being forced to live in a horse trailer—a cage determined by USDA definition as "minimum." It happened to two African lions in Ohio, Lambert and Lacy, who were kept in a tiny trailer by their well-meaning owner who did not have the resources to properly care for them.

In Florida, the minimum standards set by the Wildlife Conservation Commission allows two tigers to spend their lives in two hundred square feet, which, as Howard Baskin of Big Cat Rescue points out, is smaller than a typical parallel parking space. The USDA's federal rule doesn't specify number of feet required, leaving this judgment up to inspectors. Baskin thinks this means that the Florida minimum gets used as the federal standard, pointing out that it's the equivalent of sentencing a human being to living a life in a small bathroom. The Global Federation of Sanctuaries, which sets standards for accredited sanctuaries, requires a 1,200-square-foot minimum for a big cat enclosure to be humane—six times Florida's legal minimum.

Howard and Carole Baskin are two of a growing number of animal advocates who contend that the only solution to the abuse of big cats is a ban on private ownership. "Trying to 'regulate' the conditions under which the cats are kept by private owners is simply impossible," Howard says. "This has been proven by years of experience despite good intentions by enforcement officials."

He estimates that there are some 10,000 big cats privately owned in the U.S., with only a small percentage of these in accredited zoos and sanctuaries. He says there are 680 facilities with USDA licenses to use the big cats commercially, which means breeding, selling, or exhibiting. "No one knows how many other owners have them as pets and do not have USDA licenses. The same inspectors who monitor big cat facilities are also charged with inspecting pet stores, dog, cat, and other pet breeders and dealers, farms, slaughterhouses, laboratories, and other animal-related businesses. There are only about eighty to a hundred inspectors charged with monitoring more than 10,000 such facilities. It is financially impractical to have enough inspectors to inspect all these facilities regularly."

Finally, there is the Big Cat Safety Act, which does prohibit private ownership, although as of early 2019, the act has not passed. This act seems a no-brainer, but individuals and groups that need private ownership and backyard breeding to continue their business continue the fight to block its passage.

This act would stop ambassador big cat abuse by not allowing human/big cat interactions with the public. Without the exploiting of young big cats for pay-to-play or photo opportunities, there is no reason for the private breeding of big cat cubs. Accredited AZA zoos stopped the unregulated breeding of white tigers in their facilities in 2011.

They had been warned as far back as 1983 by William Conway, then director of the New York Zoological Society. He said showing white tigers harmed the integrity of zoos by appealing to their customers' fascination with what he called "freaks." White tigers, he said were freaks. "It's not the role of a zoo to show two-headed calves and white tigers," he said. His warning went unheeded until 2008. AZA then issued a request to their members to stop breeding white tigers. In 2011, the AZA formally adopted that stance as a policy.

Conway was attacked by Ed Maruska, director of the Cincinnati Zoo, as well as other zoos that were making huge profits off white tigers. Maruska, of course, was the original link between white tigers in accredited zoos and private ownership, which largely occurred after his zoo sold Vegas entertainers Siegfried and Roy their first white tigers.

When the AZA stops the practice of breeding, exhibition, and exploitation of white tigers but well-loved animal 'conservationist' Jack Hanna continues to exhibit them on the *Late Show with David Letterman*, going against his own AZA (Columbus Zoo) rules, we have a serious problem that the existing laws cannot stop. Jack, David, Jarod, and others believe they are above the law.

Laws do work, but there are too many loopholes in the current legislation. When Jack Hanna, a 'conservationist' who absolutely knows better, can get a tiger cub from a backyard breeder in Ohio, take it on several TV shows, pass it around at VIP/pay-to-play parties, then dump it back to that backyard breeder, we have a major negative situation for hundreds of big cat cubs used in the last thirty years. The Big Cat Public Safety Act (H.R. 1818) will stop the unregulated breeding by private people. It will stop ownership of big cats by private owners, thus protecting local police, fire, EMS, and animal control officers who must respond to their escapes, attacks on people, and other natural disasters where a big cat might endanger either officers or the public. It will also protect the current big cats in captivity and, in a way, protect future big cats by stopping any further breeding.

What is really hard to believe is that the AZA zoos, with the exception of a few, will not support the act in a written manner. On the phone, they all know it is the right thing to do, but the pressure and power from Jack Hanna stops them in their tracks.

We have everyone from the National Sheriffs' Association to the American Bar Association supporting the act but not the group that originally put big cats into private owner's hands—the AZA. Ron Kagan, CEO of the Detroit Zoo, is the most vocal supporter of the Big Cat Public Safety Act. Ron and I spoke at the Big Cat Public Safety Act congressional briefing in Washington, DC, and he said the AZA zoos should have been first to support this important act.

They're the educators and conservationists and should support the protection of big cats. Ron is brave to step up, but he is a rarity. And so it's a nightmare to try and protect big cats in the U.S. I went to Washington, D.C., to speak to senators and congressmen/congresswomen and enlist their support of the Big Cat Public Safety Act. IFAW (International Fund for Animal Welfare) and Big Cat Rescue set up the congressional briefing and it was well received.

I was therefore surprised when I went back to Washington a few months later to gain more support for the act and discovered that every time we came to support the act, Jack Hanna and other 'conservationists' came behind us a few weeks later, trying to discredit us and block passage of the act. It was not only *our* lobbyist telling us this but other congressmen/congresswomen and senators. Those who are against the act have the money and the public/celebrity support. We have only the truth.

Every time I speak in front of lawmakers and politicians I ask, "How have the current laws been working?" Things are worse for the animals. The current laws actually help the animal exploiters continue their cruel business, unchecked. If they get checked, it is a small fine or a slap on the hand. If good people expose the abuse, they are destroyed on the internet, threatened to be sued, discredited, or just plain threatened.

How do you stop White Magic?

Contact your lawmakers and demand they pass the Big Cat Public Safety Act.

EPILOGUE
The Curse

I chose the title of this book—*White Magic*—after I began investigating the white tiger phenomena in the U.S. Growing up in Ohio near the Cincinnati Zoo, I basically grew up with the white tigers. I saw the original white tigers every year and was caught up in their mystique. As I was doing research for this book, I discovered that there were no books telling the whole story, both positive and negative, of white tigers.

The only books were fluff pieces about how beautiful and rare they are, mostly eye-popping photos, perfectly posed and lighted, with very little text. If I wanted real information, I would have to go to research papers and data by white tiger experts. This led me to working with the world's foremost tiger experts in the U.S., India, and Nepal. I read their papers, articles, research, and websites as well as personally talking to them.

As I was compiling the data, interviewing both the good guys and the bad guys (as well as the gray-thinking guys), I learned that these beautiful, misunderstood big cats are cursed. "Something that brings or causes great trouble or harm, damned," the dictionary tells us, and no other words express better the history and future of the white tiger in America. And it is not the only one cursed in this equation; it has reached the people who exploit, rescue, and relocate, as well as the unknowing public.

In the process of writing this book the most successful tiger breeder in the country, Joe Schreibvogel, alias

Joe Exotic, also known as the Tiger King, was arrested on murder-for-hire and endangered species violations (killing his unwanted tigers and burying them in a secret grave). I have introduced the reader to Joe, but his thumbing his nose at laws, regulations, and the many violations/citations he received has finally caught up with him. Joe thought he was invincible, or as he has said to me before, "above the law." But the curse got him, too: he was successfully sued for a million dollars, arrested for murder-for-hire by the FBI, and has nineteen charges against him in the deaths of tigers at his facility.

The title of an article in *Mel Magazine* in 2018—"Joe Exotic: a cautionary tale...."—written about Joe's demise explains it all: "His Reign of Error, however, finally came to an end this week with his failed murder-for-hire plot against Carole Baskin, the CEO of Big Cat Sanctuary," said the magazine. "The animal sanctuary posted the still from a video Joe Exotic made that featured him threatening to shoot an effigy of Baskin, marked BCR (Big Cat Rescue) and a representative from PETA, who also challenged how Joe Exotic treated the animals in his care. Between 2009 and 2010, the Department of Agriculture documented that twenty-three tiger cubs died at his roadside zoo...."

Finally, the public, too, has been cursed. The general person's only information and "education" about white tigers comes from watching their favorite animal 'conservationists' on TV talk/entertainment shows. People watch Discovery/Animal Planet/National Geographic Wild channels with such exciting titles as "Man vs. Puma" or "Man vs. Nature." The titles say it all. Why man versus pumas or nature? It should be "Man Observing Nature" or "Man Leaves Pumas Alone in the Wild." We should be part of nature, not obnoxious outsiders. But this is how the public is being educated about wildlife.

When it comes to white tigers, the average person only sees them as props for TV 'conservationists,' magicians, and commercial products. Because of their rarity, white tigers are not filmed in the wild. TV shows do not tell the true story of their plight, only how beautiful they are. The truth about them seems antithetical to the ratings.

The abuse would stop, if only the public knew what really happens to them, but it would also destroy the white tiger business. The public's curse is believing the exploiters. They are also cursed when they discover they have been lied to, and that they have been part of the exploitation of the big cats they loved so much.

This happened after my colleagues got legislation passed to stop the capture from the wild and unnecessary breeding of orcas. We had all helped educate the public about the disgusting business of exploiting orcas. There are thousands of tigers in nonaccredited facilities across the U.S.; there are only seventy-one orcas in captivity in eight different countries. When the public learned of the truth they felt they had been betrayed by Jack Hanna and other trusted 'conservationists.' The curse of the orcas was lifted from their hearts by the truth. Their guilt of believing these 'conservationists' and supporting the abuse by going to SeaWorld disappeared as they are now fighting to stop the madness. The curse has been redirected to the real bad guys.

The Orca legislation has proved that the truth is something we can tell the public, and they can make up their own minds what to do with it. In over forty-five years of experience working with these animals, I have learned that the public deserves the truth. The truth may hurt at first but will ultimately free you.

There is no truly happy ending for the white tigers. Yes, some go to beautiful sanctuaries with amazing care, but they are not free. They still have physical and mental problems from being abused and severely inbred. Usually, they do not live a healthy life span, and they are in some form of discomfort and pain from their experiences with past owners—diet deficiencies, beatings, skeletal deformities, etc. These innocent tigers are the true victims of the curse, but the rescuers/relocators and the people who care for them for the rest of their lives are also cursed. They are cursed for loving these big cats.

As a police officer/firefighter/EMT-paramedic, I saw what evil things people can do to other people. I live with these memories every day of my life. But seeing a mature white tiger in a basement in Ohio, one who's never been out in the sunlight since he was a cub, weighing under two hundred pounds when he should be close to five hundred, has cursed me for life.

The rescuers/relocators and sanctuary personnel have had their lives changed forever. I have shed tears with these true big cat heroes and I understand their pain both emotionally and physically. They have been cursed, too. Theirs is to see these beautiful victims every day, knowing many will die young. Watching the ones that have been horribly abused try to learn to stop walking in a twenty-foot circle when they have acres in which to run.

These big cat warriors will never be able to stop helping; they will never forget what they have seen or felt. We all know a toll has been taken on our personal lives. Families and loved ones will never understand us, and sometimes I hope they never will. For why curse them?

When all is said and written, it is still not done. The story has reached its end but not its resolution, and there's still something that doesn't quite fit into the narrative arc. Life isn't always straightforward and simple and not everything can be tied up in a pretty bow. Not every story has a happy ending. The title, *White Magic*, should now be self-explanatory.

An epilogue is intended to be the summary of the book, but how do you summarize the horrific story of white tigers in the U.S.? How do we end the book when every day we receive more and more reports of white tiger births, sales, abuses, deaths, and disappearances. Almost every day, we hear in the news about another tiger either escaping or mauling another of its intended masters.

The curse of the white tigers began with Mohini being taken from her native land and brought to the U.S. and continued with the public wanting to pay-to-play with white tigers. Nora, Nikita, Como, and Yuki were in the long line that followed. The story of white tigers is a tragic tale. However, with legislation—such as the Big Cat Public Safety Act—accredited sanctuaries and AZA zoos are cleaning up the mess and giving tigers the respect and care they deserve. There could be a happy ending.

It is not the fault of the tigers that they are here, but it is our fault if we do nothing to help them. And if you truly love the white tigers, please do not love them to death.

APPENDIX
References

Chapter One
1. http://circusnospin.blogspot.com/2008/10/mohini-enchantress-mohan-x.html
2. https://www.indiatimes.com/news/india/this-is-the-story-of-mohan-the-majestic-ancestor-of-all-the-white-bengal-tigers-alive-today-253948.html
3. http://www.kamaliacademy.com/a-caged-tiger-free-to-roam/
4. http://circusnospin.blogspot.com/2008/10/mohini-enchantress-mohan-x.html
5. Rovner, Sandy, "A star is dead," The *Washington Post*, April 3, 1979
6. Reed, Theodore H., "Enchantress: Queen of an Indian palace rare white tigress comes to Washington," *National Geographic*, May 1961

Chapter Two
1. Hale, Tom, "The dark truth about white tigers," IFLScience, March 28, 2018
2. Luo, Shu-Jin, and Xiao Xu, "Save the White Tigers," *Scientific American*, October 16, 2014
3. https://www.nationalgeographic.com/science/phenomena/2013/05/23/tiger-tiger-burning-bright-just-one-gene-to-make-it-white/
4. Quammen, David, *Wild Thoughts from Wild Places*, New York: Scribner, 1998
5. "Detailed history of the white tiger," *All About Tigers*—http://allaboutwhitetigers.com/wt04.html

6. "The 20 greatest shows in Las Vegas history," *Las Vegas Weekly*, November 17, 2016
7. Beach, Sharyn, "White tigers: conserving a lie," *Advocacy for Animals*, February 8, 2010
8. "All white tigers are inbred and are not purebred," *Big Cat Rescue*
9. https://bigcatrescue.org/abuse-issues/issues/white-tigers/
10. "The truth about white tigers," crownridgetigers.com
11. http://crownridgetigers.com/the-truth-about-white-tigers
12. Nasser, Carney Anne, "Welcome to the Jungle: How Loopholes in the Federal Endangered Species Act and Animal Welfare Act are Feeding a Tiger Crisis in America," *Albany Government Law Review*, Vol. 9, April 22, 2016
13. Astaiza, Randy, "White tigers are man-made genetic freaks," *Business Insider*, December 13, 2012
14. "All white tigers are inbred and are not purebred," bigcatrescue.org
15. https://bigcatrescue.org/abuse-issues/issues/white-tigers/
16. "Tiger that injured Roy of Siegfried & Roy dies," *Associated Press*, March 26, 2014

Chapter Three

1. "Welcome to the Jungle: How Loopholes in the Federal Endangered Species Act and Animal Welfare Act are Feeding a Tiger Crisis in America," *Albany Government Law Review*, Vol. 9, April 22, 2016
2. Nyhus, Philip, and Ron L. Tilson, "The conservation value of tigers: separating science from fiction," *Journal of the WildCat Conservation Legal Aid Society*, Vol. I, Summer 2009
3. Jeffrey, James, "Does the U.S. have a pet tiger problem?" *BBC News*, June 11, 2018

4. "U.S. captive-bred inter-subspecific crossed or generic tigers," *U.S. Fish and Wildlife Service*, https://www.fws.gov/home/feature/2016/pdfs/Generic-Tiger-Final-Rule-FAQs.pdf
5. Nyhus, Philip, and Ron. L. Tilson, "The conservation value of tigers: separating science from fiction," *Faculty Scholarship Program*, 2009
6. https://digitalcommons.colby.edu/faculty_scholarship/51

Chapter Four
1. Landers, Jackson, "Why white tigers should go extinct," *Slate*, December 13, 2012
2. https://slate.com/technology/2012/12/white-tiger-controversy-zoos-shouldnt-raise-these-inbred-ecologically-irrelevant-animals.html
3. ("Welfare and conservation implications of intentional breeding for the expression of rare recessive alleles," Association of Zoos & Aquariums, Animal Welfare Committee: Task Force on Animal Breeding Practices, June 2011)
4. "Paw Project founder Jennifer Conrad and tiger Diablo," Big Cat Rescue, April 4, 2009– https://bigcatrescue.org/paw-project-founder-jennifer-conrad-and-tiger-diablo/
5. Prendergast, Alan, "The cruelest cut," Houston Press, September 11, 2013
6. Bates, Karl Leif, "The bigger the animal, the stiffer the shoes," Science Daily, February 25, 2010
7. "All white tigers are inbred and are not purebred," Big Cat Rescue
8. https://bigcatrescue.org/abuse-issues/issues/white-tigers/
9. Laughlin, Dr. Dan, "The white tiger fraud," https://bigcatrescue.org/the-white-tiger-fraud/

Chapter Five
1. O'Connor, Jennifer, "The suffering is over at the Hawthorn Corporation!" PETA, November 30, 2017
2. https://www.peta.org/blog/hideous-hawthorn-corporation-history/
3. Kaufman, Marc, "USDA seizes circus elephants," *Washington Post*, March 18, 2004

Chapter Six
1. Somaiya, Ravi, "Inside America's tiger-breeding farms," *Newsweek*, July 28, 2010
2. "The white tiger myth," tigersinamerica.org
3. http://www.tigersinamerica.org/whitetiger.htm
4. Lavery, Jimmy, Jim Mydlach and Louis Mydlach, *The Secret Life of Siegfried and Roy: How the Tiger King Tamed Las Vegas*, Beverly Hills: Phoenix Books, 2008
5. Harrigan, Stephen, *The Eye of the Mammoth: Selected Essays*, Austin: University of Texas Press, 2013

Chapter Seven
1. "Conservation Game" Tim Harrison-Outreach for Animals and Nightly Entertainment, Documentary-2021
2. Heimbuch, Jaymi, "What is an ambassador animal?" MNN.com, September 29, 2015
3. Harrison, Tim. *Wildlife Warrior: More Tales From Suburban Safaris*. Orange Frazer Press, 2006

Chapter Eight
1. "Conservation Game" Tim Harrison-Outreach for Animals and Nightly Entertainment, Documentary-2021

Chapter Nine
1. "Tasha the cougar and Nikita the tigress call TWS home," *The Wildcat Sanctuary*, April 5, 2012

Chapter Ten
1. Ruzek, Tim, "Fate of Siberian tiger in question," *Minnesota Post Bulletin*, July 24, 2001
2. Laurence, Charles, "Police probe couple who sold 400lb tiger found in Harlem flat," *The (British) Daily Telegraph*, October 12, 2003
3. McMillion, Scott, "Owner of 'animal actors' indicted on federal charges," *Bozeman Daily Chronicle*, August 27, 2004
4. Silver, Beth, "Exotic animal merchant sentenced," *Pioneer (Twin Cities) Press*, October 5, 2005
5. "What ever happened to the highly publicized case of Como the white tiger?" wildcatsantuary.org, April 25, 2016
6. https://www.wildcatsanctuary.org/what-ever-happened-to-como-the-white-tiger/
7. Thies, Tammy, "The box read: 'Interstate Meat Dist., Inc.,'" *Uproar magazine*, April 15, 2016

Chapter Eleven
1. "2 Chainz spends $300,000 on wedding," *Florida Sentinel Bulletin*, August 20, 2018
2. Bueno, Antoinette, "Kaley Cuoco celebrates her 30th birthday with her sister, furry friends," ET, November 30, 2015
3. Knibbs, Kate, "This celebrity-studded Instagram petting zoo is a disaster waiting to happen," gizmodo.com, January 15, 2016

Chapter Twelve
1. Enden, David, "Big Cats: Available in Backyards Nationwide," TEDxCSU, March 22, 2017
2. Dotson, J. Dianne, "The role of tigers in the ecosystem," sciencing.com, April 30, 2018
3. Vince, Gaia, "Tigers: can we afford to save them?" bbc.com, March 20, 2012

Chapter Thirteen
1. Campbell, Charlie, "Traditional Chinese medical authorities are unable to stop the booming trade in rare animal parts," *Time*, November 22, 2016
2. Fischer, Hank, Wolf Wars, Guilford, CT: Falcon Guides, 1995

Chapter Fourteen
1. Merrett, Robyn, "Oklahoma zookeeper 'Joe Exotic' indicted for alleged murder-for-hire," *People*, September 11, 2018
2. Smith, Jennifer, "Tiger zoo owner who calls himself 'Joe Exotic' arrested," *Daily Mail*, September 10, 2018
3. Hanson, Hilary, "Animal sanctuary owner says she was target in zookeeper's murder-for-hire plot," *Huffington Post*, September 9, 2018
4. Olmstead, Molly, "Oklahoma zookeeper known as 'Joe Exotic' charged in murder-for-hire plot, Slate, September 10, 2018
5. Swenson, Kyle, "Exotic-tiger-zoo owner ranted for years about an animal rights activist who now says he tried to have her killed," *The Washington Post*, September 10, 2018
6. "Joe Exotic arrested for murder for hire," bigcatrescue.org, December 26, 2018

7. https://bigcatrescue.org/joe-exotic-arrested-murder-hire/.
8. Clay, Nolan, "Former Oklahoma zookeeper Joe Exotic to stay locked up," *The Oklahoman*, October 4, 2018
9. Merrett, Robyn, "Oklahoma zookeeper 'Joe Exotic' indicted for alleged murder-for-hire," *People*, September 11, 2018
10. "Joe Exotic arrested for murder for hire," bigcatrescue.org, September 11, 2018 https://bigcatrescue.org/joe-exotic-arrested-murder-hire/

Chapter Fifteen
1. "Zanesville massacre: 18 tigers, 17 lions, 3 cougars gunned down," Big Cat Rescue, January 27, https://bigcatrescue.org/zanesville-massacre-18-tigers-17-lions-3-cougars-gunned-down/
2. "2019 update on murder for hire," bigcatrescue.org, January 10, 2019
3. https://bigcatrescue.org/joe-exotic-arrested-murder-hire/
4. "New York JnK tiger rescue," bigcatrescue.org, January 23, 2019
5. https://bigcatrescue.org/jnk/

Chapter Sixteen
1. "Foreign Species and the U.S. Endangered Species Act," *U.S. Fish & Wildlife Service* https://www.fws.gov/international/pdf/factsheet-endangered-species-act-foreign-species.pdf
2. Baskin, Howard, "Why regulating conditions under which big cats are kept simply does not and cannot work," bigcatrescue.org, August 10, 2018
3. "Today at Big Cat Rescue AZA says no more white tigers," bigcatrescue.org, April 2, 2012

4. "Welfare and conservation implications of intentional breeding for the expression of rare recessive alleles," *Association of Zoos & Aquariums*, June 2011

Epilogue

1. Burnett III, Zach, "Joe Exotic: a cautionary tale of a murder-for-hire plot involving tigers, Michael Jackson's pet alligators, and, of course, a Florida man," *MEL magazine*, 2018 "https://melmagazine.com/en-us/story/joe-exotic-a-cautionary-tale-of-a-murder-for-hire-plot-involving-tigers-michael-jacksons-pet

LEGISLATION

Animal Welfare Act: https://www.nal.usda.gov/awic/animal-welfare-act

The Animal Welfare Act was signed into law in 1966. It is the only Federal law in the United States that regulates the treatment of animals in research, exhibition, transport, and by dealers. Other laws, policies, and guidelines may include additional species coverage or specifications for animal care and use, but all refer to the Animal Welfare Act as the minimum acceptable standard.

Federal Endangered Species Act: https://www.fws.gov/international/laws-treaties-agreements/us-conservation-laws/endangered-species-act.html

A key legislation for both domestic and international conservation. The act aims to provide a framework to conserve and protect endangered and threatened species and their habitats.

H.R. 1818–Big Cat Public Safety Act: https://www.whyanimalsdothething.com/legislation-breakdown-1818-bigcatpublicsafety/

H.R. 1818 is a proposed bill to amend the Captive Wildlife Safety Act, which is itself an amendment of the Lacey Act. The CWSA made illegal the importing, exporting, buying, selling, transporting, receiving, and/or acquiring big cats across state or federal borders. It also exempted any USDA-licensed institution from such restrictions. H.R. 1818 goes further, preventing all non-commercial ownership of big cats and hugely restricts which USDA-licensed commercial facilities can house, transport, and breed big cats.

H. R. 1818

To amend the Lacey Act Amendments of 1981 to clarify provisions enacted by the Captive Wildlife Safety Act, to further the conservation of certain wildlife species, and for other purposes.

IN THE HOUSE OF REPRESENTATIVES

MARCH 30, 2017

Mr. DENHAM (for himself, Mr. JONES, Mr. FARENTHOLD, Mr. LOBIONDO, Mr. GAETZ, Ms. TSONGAS, Mr. ROSS, and Mr. JOHNSON of Ohio) introduced the following bill; which was referred to the Committee on Natural Resources

A BILL

To amend the Lacey Act Amendments of 1981 to clarify provisions enacted by the Captive Wildlife Safety Act, to further the conservation of certain wildlife species, and for other purposes.

Be it enacted by the Senate and House of Representatives of the United States of America in Congress assembled,

SECTION 1. SHORT TITLE.

This Act may be cited as the "Big Cat Public Safety Act."

SECTION 2. DEFINITIONS.

(a) IN GENERAL.—Section 2 of the Lacey Act Amendments of 1981 (16 U.S.C. 3371) is amended—

(1) by redesignating subsections (a) through (k) as subsections (b) through (l), respectively; and

(2) by inserting before subsection (b) (as so redesignated) the following:

"(a) BREED.–The term 'breed' means to facilitate propagation or reproduction (whether intentionally or negligently), or to fail to prevent propagation or reproduction.".

(b) CONFORMING AMENDMENTS.–

(1) CONSOLIDATED FARM AND RURAL DEVELOPMENT ACT.– Section 349(a)(3) of the Consolidated Farm and Rural Development Act (7 U.S.C. 1997(a)(3)) is amended by striking "section 2(a)" and inserting "section 2(b)".

(2) LACEY ACT AMENDMENTS OF 1981.–

(A) Section 3(e)(2)(C) of the Lacey Act Amendments of 1981 (16 U.S.C. 3372(e)(2)(C)) is amended–

(i) in clause (ii), by striking "section 2(g)" and inserting "section 2(h)"; and

(ii) in clause (iii), by striking "section 2(g)" and inserting "section 2(h)".

(B) Section 7(c) of the Lacey Act Amendments of 1981 (16 U.S.C. 3376(c)) is amended by striking "section 2(f)(2)(A)" and inserting "section 2(g)(2)(A)".

SECTION 3. PROHIBITIONS.

Section 3 of the Lacey Act Amendments of 1981 (16 U.S.C. 3372) is amended–

(1) in subsection (a)–

(A) in paragraph (2)–

(i) in subparagraph (A), by striking the semicolon at the end and inserting "; or";

(ii) in subparagraph (B)(iii), by striking "; or" and inserting a semicolon; and

(iii) by striking subparagraph (C); and

(B) in paragraph (4), by striking "(1) through (3)" and inserting "(1) through (3) or subsection (e)"; and

(2) by amending subsection (e) to read as follows:

"(e) CAPTIVE WILDLIFE OFFENSE.—

"(1) IN GENERAL.—It is unlawful for any person to import, export, transport, sell, receive, acquire, or purchase in interstate or foreign commerce, or in a manner substantially affecting interstate or foreign commerce, or to breed or possess, any prohibited wildlife species.

"(2) LIMITATION ON APPLICATION.—Paragraph (1) does not apply to—

"(A) an entity exhibiting animals to the public under a Class C license from the Department of Agriculture and that holds such license in good standing, if the entity—

"(i) has not been, and does not employ any person engaged in animal care who has been, convicted of or fined for an offense involving the abuse or neglect of any animal pursuant to any State, local, or Federal law;

"(ii) has not had, and does not employ any person who has had, a license or permit regarding the care, possession, exhibition, breeding, or sale of animals revoked or suspended by any State, local, or Federal agency, including the Department of Agriculture, within the preceding 3-year period;

"(iii) has not been cited by the Department of Agriculture under the Animal Welfare Act (7 U.S.C. 2131 et seq.) within the preceding 12-month period for any repeat violation for—

"(I) inadequate veterinary care;

"(II) handling that causes stress or trauma or a threat to public safety;

"(III) insufficient provisions of food or water; or

"(IV) failure to allow facility inspection;

"(iv) does not allow any individual other than a trained professional employee or contractor of the licensee (or an accompanying employee receiving professional training) or a licensed veterinarian (or an accompanying veterinary student) to come into direct physical contact with a prohibited wildlife species;

"(v) ensures that during public exhibition of a lion (Panthera leo), tiger (Panthera tigris), leopard (Panthera pardus), snow leopard (Uncia uncia), jaguar (Panthera onca), cougar (Puma concolor), or any hybrid thereof, the animal is at least 15 feet from members of the public unless there is a permanent barrier that prevents public contact or risk of contact;

"(vi) does not breed any prohibited wildlife species unless the breeding is conducted pursuant to a species-specific, publicly available, peer-reviewed population management plan developed according to established conservation science principles;

"(vii) maintains liability insurance in an amount of not less than $250,000 for each occurrence of property damage, bodily injury, or death caused by any prohibited wildlife species possessed by the person; and

"(viii) has a written plan that is made available to local law enforcement, State agencies and Federal agencies on request, for the quick and safe recapture or destruction of prohibited wildlife species in the event a prohibited wildlife species escapes, including, but not limited to, written protocols for training staff on methods of safe recapture of the escaped prohibited wildlife species;

"(B) a State college, university, or agency, or State-licensed veterinarian;

"(C) a wildlife sanctuary that cares for prohibited wildlife species, and—

"(i) is a corporation that is exempt from taxation under section 501(a) of the Internal Revenue Code of 1986 and described in sections 501(c)(3) and 170(b)(1)(A)(vi) of such Code;

"(ii) does not commercially trade in prohibited wildlife species, including offspring, parts, and byproducts of such animals;

"(iii) does not breed the prohibited wildlife species;

"(iv) does not allow direct contact between the public and prohibited wildlife species; and

"(v) does not allow the transportation and display of prohibited wildlife species off-site;

"(D) has custody of the prohibited wildlife species solely for the purpose of expeditiously transporting the prohibited wildlife species to a person described in this paragraph with respect to the species; or

"(E) an entity or individual that is in possession of a prohibited wildlife species that was born before the date of the enactment of the Big Cat Public Safety Act, and—

"(i) not later than 180 days after the date of the enactment of the Big Cat Public Safety Act, the entity or individual registers each individual animal of each prohibited wildlife species with the United States Fish and Wildlife Service;

"(ii) does not breed, acquire, or sell any prohibited wildlife species after the date of the enactment of such Act; and

"(iii) does not allow direct contact between the public and prohibited wildlife species.".

SECTION 4. PENALTIES.

(a) CIVIL PENALTIES.—Section 4(a)(1) of the Lacey Act Amendments of 1981 (16 U.S.C. 3373(a)(1)) is amended—

(1) by inserting "(e)," after "(d),"; and

(2) by inserting ", (e)," after "subsection (d)".

(b) CRIMINAL PENALTIES.—Section 4(d) of the Lacey Act Amendments of 1981 (16 U.S.C. 3373(d)) is amended—

(1) in paragraph (1)(A), by inserting "(e)," after "(d),";

(2) in paragraph (1)(B), by inserting "(e)," after "(d),";

(3) in paragraph (2), by inserting "(e)," after "(d),"; and

(4) by adding at the end the following:

"(4) Any person who knowingly violates subsection (e) of section 3 shall be fined not more than $20,000, or imprisoned for not more than five years, or both. Each violation shall be a separate offense and the offense shall be deemed to have been committed not only in the district where the violation first occurred, but also in any district in which the defendant may have taken or been in possession of the prohibited wildlife species.".

SECTION 5. FORFEITURE OF PROHIBITED WILDLIFE SPECIES.

Section 5(a)(1) of the Lacey Act Amendments of 1981 (16 U.S.C. 3374(a)(1)) is amended by inserting "bred, possessed," before "imported, exported,".

SECTION 6. ADMINISTRATION.

Section 7(a) of the Lacey Act Amendments of 1981 (16 U.S.C. 3376(a)) is amended by adding at the end the following:

"(3) The Secretary shall, in consultation with other relevant Federal and State agencies, promulgate any regulations necessary to implement section 3(e).".

INFORMED SOURCES, ORGANIZATIONS, AND SANCTUARIES

AZA (Association of Zoos & Aquariums)
Silver Springs, MD
PH: 301.562.0777 (M–F, 8:30AM–5:30PM EST)
http://www.aza.org
The oldest conservation entity, formed in 1924, and today is active in education, conservation, and research. It's also the accrediting agency for zoos and aquariums, ensuring that accredited facilities meet high standards of animal care. Through the Species Survival Plans and Population Management Plans, it works to manage genetically diverse captive populations of various animal species.

Black Pine Animal Sanctuary
1426 W 300 N, P.O. Box 02, Albion, IN 46701
PH: 260.636.7383
E-mail: info@blackpine.org
https://www.bpsanctuary.org

Big Cat Rescue
12802 Easy St, Tampa, FL 33625
PH: 813.920.4130
E-mail: info@bigcatrescue.org
https://bigcatrescue.org
All visits must be reserved and pre-paid here:
   https://bigcatrescue.org/tickets

Big Cat Sanctuary Alliance
Contact via their website at: https://www.bigcatalliance.org/

Bronx Zoo
2300 Southern Blvd, Bronx, NY 10460
PH: 718.367.1010
https://bronxzoo.com/

Cincinnati Zoo & Botanical Gardens
3400 Vine St, Cincinnati, OH 45220
PH: 513.281.4700
cincinnatizoo.org

Columbus Zoo & Aquarium
4850 Powell Rd, Powell, OH 43065
PH: 614.645.3400
https://www.columbuszoo.org

The Global Federation for Animal Sanctuaries
https://www.sanctuaryfederation.org/
Begun in 2007 when animal protection leaders recognized the difficulty in identifying true sanctuaries among the wide array of animal care facilities around the world, and its mission is to "better recognize and support sanctuaries that are dedicated to providing excellent animal care. It's the only globally recognized organization for certifying that a facility meets the GFAS Standards of Excellence and recognizes those as a true sanctuary.

International Fund for Animal Welfare
https://www.ifaw.org/united-states
The IFAW, one of the largest animal welfare and conservation charities in the world, rescues animals, safeguards populations and habitat, and serves as an advocate for animal protections.

Lions, Tigers, and Bears Sanctuary
24402 Martin Way, Alpine, CA 91901
PH: 619.659.8078
FAX: 619.659.8841
https://lionstigersandbears.org

Minnesota Zoo & Aquarium
13000 Zoo Blvd
Apple Valley, MN 55124
PH: 952.431.9200
mnzoo.org

New Delhi Zoo
Mathura Road, New Delhi, Delhi 110002, India
PH: +91 11 2435 8500
nzpnewdelhi.gov.in

Smithsonian National Museum of Natural History
10th St & Constitution Ave, NW, Washington, DC 20560
PH: 202.633.1000
https://naturalhistory.si.edu

Smithsonian National Zoological Park
3001 Connecticut Ave NW, Washington, DC 20008
PH: 202.633.4888
https://nationalzoo.si.edu

TigersinAmerica.org
A site dedicated to succinct information on all aspects of tigers, from bad laws, private owners, and roadside zoos to conservation.

Tiger Haven, Inc.
237 Harvey Rd, Kingston, Tennessee 37763
PH: 865.376.4100
www.tigerhaven.org

Turpentine Creek Wildlife Refuge
239 Turpentine Creek Lane, Eureka Springs, Arkansas 72632
PH: 479.253.5841
E-mail: tigers@turpentinecreek.org
https://turpentinecreek.org

USDA APHIS Database
https://www.aphis.usda.gov/aphis/ourfocus/animalwelfare/sa_awa/awa-inspection-and-annual-reports
A documentation of animal facilities across the U.S., showing if they have been cited by USDA for violations of the Animal Welfare Act, and what those violations were.

WildCat Ridge Sanctuary
PO Box 280, Scotts Mills, OR 97375
PH: 503.873.2309
http://www.wildcatridgesanctuary.org/

Wild Animal Sanctuary
2999 Co Rd 53, Keenesburg, CO 80643
PH: 303.536.0118
https://www.wildanimalsanctuary.org/

The Wildcat Sanctuary
P.O. Box 314, Sandstone, MN 55072
PH: 320.245.6871
E-mail: info@wildcatsanctuary.org
https://www.wildcatsanctuary.org/

Zoological Association of America, Analytic Report of Standards, Practices, and Facilities https://bigcatrescue.org/wp-content/uploads/2017/04/HSUS-2017-03-03_ZAA-Factsheet.pdf
A rigidly documented analysis of the ZAA, the premise being that the ZAA "severely weakens laws and regulations intended to restrict the private possession of dangerous wild animals to only qualified facilities."

ABOUT THE AUTHORS

TIM HARRISON is a retired Police Officer/Firefighter/EMT-Paramedic, City of Oakwood (near Dayton, OH.) Currently an Adjunct Instructor for TEEX/NERRTC (National Emergency Response and Recovery Center) at Disaster City/EOTC, Texas A&M University. Author of *Wild Times, Tales from Suburban Safaris*, and *Wildlife Warrior, More Tales from Suburban Safaris* chronicling over 45 years of rescuing, relocating, and caring for dangerous wild/exotic animals. Tim is the subject of the award-winning documentaries, *The Elephant in the Living Room* and *Conservation Game*, which features his work with his non-profit organization, Outreach for Animals. Tim has been highlighted in magazines and on television shows such as *National Geographic Magazine*, *Rolling Stone Magazine*, *Time for Kids*, ABC's *20/20* TV show, Animal Planet, Discovery Channel, Dr. Oz *True Crimes*, Sunday Night (Australia), National Geographic Wild Channel, and TV Tokyo. His mission is to teach proper behavior around wildlife. (Learn more about Tim at www.humananimaladvocate.com)

WILLIAM F. RANDOLPH, JR.—known simply as Bill to his friends and family—has worked in various public safety departments in different counties in Ohio for over twenty years before finally retiring as a special police officer from Twin Valley Behavioral Healthcare Center in Columbus, Ohio. Bill has been a friend, and sometimes co-worker, of Tim Harrison's for several of those years. Bill has written various published articles in nationally known martial arts magazines, working with another mutual friend Grandmaster Roger L. Haines. In some cases, Tim Harrison has figured prominently in these articles due to his own expansive knowledge and tenure within the world of martial arts. *White Magic* will serve as a dual milestone for Bill, being both the first time that Tim Harrison and Bill Randolph have collaborated on a project of this magnitude together as well as Bill's first published stand-alone book. Bill lives in Centerville, Ohio.